THE PRACTICAL ENCYCLOPEDIA OF

QUILTING
&QUILT DESIGN

*A complete guide to quilting, patchwork and
appliqué, with over 140 practical projects: quilts
and throws, cushions, clothing, and accessories
for every room*

ISABEL STANLEY AND JENNY WATSON

SPECIAL PHOTOGRAPHY BY GLORIA NICOL

HERMES
HOUSE

THIS EDITION PUBLISHED BY HERMES HOUSE
AN IMPRINT OF
ANNESS PUBLISHING LIMITED
HERMES HOUSE
88-89 BLACKFRIARS ROAD
LONDON SE1 8HA

A CIP CATALOGUE RECORD FOR THIS BOOK IS AVAILABLE FROM THE
BRITISH LIBRARY

PUBLISHER: JOANNA LORENZ
PROJECT EDITOR: JUDITH SIMONS
TEXT EDITOR: JUDY WALKER
PHOTOGRAPHER: GLORIA NICOL
STEP PHOTOGRAPHER: LUCY TIZARD
STYLIST: GLORIA NICOL
ASSISTANT STYLIST: EMMA HARDY
DESIGNER: LOUISE MORLEY
ILLUSTRATOR: LUCINDA GANDERTON

PREVIOUSLY PUBLISHED AS *THE ULTIMATE QUILTING AND PATCHWORK COMPANION*

© ANNESS PUBLISHING LIMITED 1996, 2000
1 3 5 7 9 10 8 6 4 2

CONTENTS
· · · · · ·

INTRODUCTION 7
TOOLS AND EQUIPMENT 8
MATERIALS 10
FABRICS 12
CHOOSING FABRICS 14
BASIC TECHNIQUES 18
· · · · · ·
HISTORIC STYLE 27
INTRODUCTION 28
PROJECTS 30
· · · · · ·
COUNTRY STYLE 81
INTRODUCTION 82
PROJECTS 84
· · · · · ·
ETHNIC STYLE 135
INTRODUCTION 136
PROJECTS 138
· · · · · ·
CONTEMPORARY STYLE 189
INTRODUCTION 190
PROJECTS 192
· · · · · ·
TEMPLATES 242
INDEX 254
ACKNOWLEDGEMENTS 256

INTRODUCTION

Quilting is a very old craft. For centuries, the Chinese have used quilted cloth for their padded winter clothing. The Crusaders discovered that the quilted shirts donned by Arabs offered ideal protection when worn beneath chainmail. They brought the idea back home as early as the 13th century when it was adapted into bedcovers by European women.

When the first pilgrims set sail for America in the 16th century the idea travelled again. Lack of resources necessitated that the settlers recycled their clothes to make quilt tops, cutting the fabric smaller and smaller each time, patching or "clouting" it, until it finally wore out. As needs must, the first quilts were practical, not pretty. However, as the settlers prospered, the pioneering plainness of the quilts and patchworks became more elaborate and colourful. A whole variety of motifs and designs evolved. Appliqué followed as a popular way of decorating the quilts, and so the patchwork quilt was born.

These timeless, ever-popular and closely related crafts are brought together here, featuring traditional techniques from all parts of the world alongside new interpretations and inspired designs from today's needlecrafters. Before starting any of the 140 varied projects featured here, do read through the introductory pages, detailing tools, equipment and materials to use, choosing and using fabrics to best effect, and the basic techniques you will need to master to produce truly professional results.

TOOLS AND EQUIPMENT
· · · · · ·

Many needleworkers will already have most of the equipment listed here. However, the more specialist items are readily available from craft shops and department stores.

SCISSORS AND CUTTING TOOLS
· · · · · ·

Dressmaker's scissors or shears Use for cutting out fabric only, so as not to dull the blades.

Paper scissors Sharpen these regularly and only use for paper.

Embroidery scissors These small, sharp and sometimes decorative scissors are used in patchwork, quilting and appliqué to cut thread and trim fabric.

Pinking shears These scissors have serrated blades and are used to prevent fraying on cut edges and also for cutting decorative edges.

Rotary cutter This tool should always be used in conjunction with a cutting mat. Use to cut out patch pieces accurately. Check blades for any nicks and replace when necessary.

Craft knife Useful for cutting out cardboard or plastic (acetate) templates. Always cut away from the body.

MEASURING TOOLS
· · · · · ·

Metal-edged ruler Use when drafting templates and also when cutting cardboard and fabric with a rotary cutter or knife.

Metre rule Use together with a set square to cut lengths of fabric.

Set square Use to measure accurate right angles and use with a metre rule to cut lengths of fabric.

Tape measure A flexible measuring tool, useful for measuring lengths of fabric.

Pair of compasses Use for drawing circles.

MARKERS
· · · · · ·

Adjustable marker and gauge A useful tool for checking measurements.

Vanishing marker Marks made with this special marker will fade on contact with water or air and therefore can be used to mark designs on to fabric. A soft lead pencil can also be used, but only on the reverse of the fabric.

Dressmaker's wheel and chalk A piece of tailor's chalk can be used directly on fabric as it will brush off later. It can also be used in conjunction with a dressmaker's wheel for pouncing (see Basic Techniques).

SEWING EQUIPMENT
· · · · · ·

Needles "Sharps" are used for hand-sewing appliqué and patchwork and "betweens" for making smaller stitches.

Crewel needles These are used for working embroidery stitches and come in sizes 1 to 10. Use size 7 for cotton and sailcloth fabrics.

Pins Discard any blunt or rusty pins. Quilting pins are longer than dressmaker's pins and pass through several layers of fabric easily.

Safety pins These are sometimes used in place of pins to hold together several layers of a quilt.

Beeswax Run the wax along quilting thread before stitching so that the thread passes smoothly though the fabric.

Thimble These are essential, especially for hand quilting where the needle has to be pushed through several layers at once.

Unpicker An essential tool used to rip out machine stitches.

Iron Essential for pressing patchwork seams. If possible, use a steam iron to press seams and remove wrinkles. Otherwise use a dry iron with a damp pressing cloth.

HOOPS AND FRAMES
· · · · · ·

Embroidery hoop Two tightly fitting rings hold the fabric taut. Plastic hoops with a metal spring closure are recommended for use under the sewing machine. Use a large wooden hoop.

Embroidery frame These four-sided frames can be either freestanding or hand-held. Fabric is tightened by adjusting the side rollers.

MISCELLANEOUS
· · · · · ·

Fabric glue This may be used in place of fusible bonding web to secure appliqué to the ground fabric.

Paper glue Spray glue is recommended for making templates.

Fabric paints and dyes Painted fabrics may be quilted and water-based non-toxic paints which are fixed by ironing are recommended. Use fabric dyes to create unusual colours, or to unify fabrics. Both hot and cold water dyes are available, although cold dyes need to be fixed. Follow the manufacturer's instructions.

KEY:
1 Dressmaker's scissors or shears
2 Embroidery scissors
3 Pinking shears
4 Rotary cutter
5 Craft knife
6 Metal-edged ruler
7 Metre rule
8 Tape measure
9 Set square
10 Pair of compasses
11 Adjustable marker and gauge
12 Vanishing marker
13 Dressmaker's chalk
14 Needles
15 Beeswax
16 Quilting pins
17 Safety pins
18 Thimble
19 Unpicker
20 Embroidery hoop
21 Large hoop for quilting
22 Fabric glue
23 Fabric paints and dyes

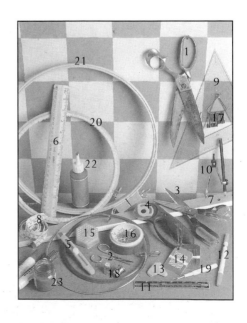

MATERIALS

Most of the following materials are standard items used regularly in needlework. More specialist items are available from craft shops or department stores.

Acid-free paper Use to wrap textiles for safe storage.

Beads and sequins Choose from a wide selection of materials, including glass, wood, plastic and bone.

Bias binding This is a narrow strip of fabric used to cover raw edges. It can be purchased ready-made or hand-made (see Basic Techniques).

Buttons Choose from a wide variety of materials, including plastic, mother-of-pearl, wood or fabric-covered. Used as fastenings for clothing, buttons can also be used for decoration or to fasten quilts and cushions.

Dressmaker's carbon paper This is used to transfer designs to fabric.

Embroidery threads Choose from pearl cotton, a high sheen 2-ply thread; stranded embroidery thread, a 5-ply thread (separate the strands for fine work); machine embroidery thread, available in various weights and a full range of colours including metallic.

Eyelets (grommets) Available in kit form, these are used to thread cord or ribbon through for a tie fastening.

Iron-on fusible bonding web This bonds two layers of fabric together and is often used to bond an appliqué motif to the ground fabric. Templates can be traced on to the backing paper.

Iron-on interfacing Lightweight interfacing can be used on the wrong side of patch pieces to mark out the seam line for machine stitching. It can also be used to back fabric.

Isometric, graph or squared dressmaker's paper Use to accurately draw a motif or template.

Lace Strips of lace or patches of lace can be used to embellish appliqué.

Press studs (snap fasteners) These metallic fasteners can be used to secure two pieces of fabric together, such as a cushion cover opening.

Ribbon This can be used to embellish appliqué or crazy patchwork or to edge a border. Choose from a variety of materials, including velvet, satin or man-made fabric.

Stuffing This is used to fill cushions and soft toys and is made from cotton, wool and synthetic fibres.

Thread For hand-sewing, use 100%

cotton thread, and for machine-sewing use 100% cotton or a polyester blend. Tacking (basting) thread is stronger than sewing thread and is used for temporarily securing layers of fabric. Quilting thread is also much stronger.

Tissue paper This is used for transferring designs and also for holding appliqué shapes together.

Tracing paper Use to trace off a design.

Trimmings These are used to make unusual edgings or to embellish a quilt or patchwork piece. Examples include fringing, pompon tape, tassels and flat ribbon tape.

Wadding (batting) This soft fabric is used as a middle layer for quilts and for filling trapunto designs. It is usually made from cotton, but is also available in silk, wool and synthetics.

Yarn Used in quilting to fill a corded quilt. It is also used for embroidery stitches and knitting.

Zip (zipper) Used to close together two open edges.

KEY:
1 Acid-free paper
2 Wadding (batting)
3 Beads and sequins
4 Bias binding
5 Buttons
6 Dressmaker's carbon paper
7 Eyelets (grommets)
8 Embroidery threads
9 Machine embroidery thread
10 Graph paper
11 Iron-on fusible bonding web
12 Iron-on interfacing
13 Lace
14 Stuffing
15 Press studs (snap fasteners)
16 Ribbon
17 Stencil card
18 Sewing thread
19 Tacking (basting) thread
20 Trimmings
21 Yarn

FABRICS

· · · · · ·

Many different types of fabric can be employed in patchwork, quilting and appliqué work. Detailed information on choosing fabric designs for your work is given in the following pages.

Calico A strong, plain-weave fabric, usually white or natural with darker flecks; available in a variety of weights.

Corduroy/needlecord (fine-wale corduroy) A plain-weave fabric with vertical pile-effect ribbing. Although it frays easily, it is suitable for appliqué and large-scale patch pieces.

Cotton Woven from the raw material, cotton is hard-wearing, and launders and presses well. Available in a wide range of plain and patterned print colours, this is the best choice for patchwork.

Felt This non-woven fabric is made from wool by compressing the fibres with moisture and heat. Felt shrinks, so is not suitable for articles that need regular washing. However, it is ideal for appliqué work as it does not fray.

Gingham Alternating stripes of coloured and white threads in the warp and weft produce this checked pattern in cotton or cotton blend fabric.

Lawn A fine crisp cotton, or cotton blend fabric, this is available in printed designs and plain colours.

Linen Woven from a natural fibre produced by the flax plant, the variable thickness of the yarn produces an uneven and attractive appearance to the fabric. Linen frays and creases easily, but is suitable as a ground fabric.

Muslin A white or natural open-weave cotton or cotton blend fabric, this is suitable for backing trapunto or corded quilts, shadow quilting and appliqué.

Organdy This fine cotton fabric is starched and is suitable for shadow work.

Organza A gauzy, crisp fabric woven from silk or synthetic fibres or a silk and synthetic blend. Available in plain colours, and with metallic and iridescent effects, it is suitable for appliqué and shadow work. It can also be used for delicate patchwork.

PVC/poly vinyl chloride (acetate) This plastic, cotton-backed cloth is not flexible like ordinary fabrics so is difficult to work with. However, it can be used for patchwork and appliqué if you lubricate your sewing machine and the machine foot before stitching.

Sateen This soft fabric has surface sheen and is more subtle than cotton or cotton blend fabrics. It is used in patchwork and is a popular choice for quilting.

Satin This shiny fabric can be woven from cotton, silk or synthetics. It frays and creases easily, but can be used to good effect in patchwork and appliqué.

Silk The queen of fabrics, silk works well for almost any project. Woven from the natural fibre produced by the silk worm, silk fabrics are lustrous and available in a wide variety of textures, colours, patterns and weights.

Shantung Woven with yarns of irregular thickness, giving an uneven surface, shantung fabric frays easily but can be used for patchwork and quilting.

Taffeta This is a plain-weave fabric with a two-tone effect. Produced in both natural and synthetic silk fibres, it is suitable for appliqué and especially effective in small patchwork.

Velvet Produced in cotton, cotton blend and synthetics, this fabric has a closely woven backing and a dense cut-pile surface. Dress velvet is lighter and more lustrous but frays easily and is difficult to handle. The fabric nap must always lie in the same direction for patchwork.

Voile This fine woven fabric is translucent and often used for shadow work. Cotton voile is finer and easier to work with than synthetic varieties.

Wool Made from woven fleece, the natural fibre has a springy texture and insulating properties. Synthetic blends mimic these properties well. However, wool does not launder easily because it is prone to shrinkage. Suitable for inlaid appliqué, light weights can also be used for patchwork.

KEY:

1 Corduroy/ needlecord (fine-wale corduroy)	7 Organza
	8 PVC/poly vinyl chloride (acetate)
2 Cotton	9 Satin
3 Felt	10 Silk
4 Gingham	11 Taffeta
5 Linen	12 Velvet
6 Organdy	13 Wool

CHOOSING FABRICS

Patchwork is traditionally made from scraps and oddments left over from past sewing projects. Way back in time, old clothes were unpicked and good patches of cloth were cut out to use. Today, however, few people make their own clothes and you may be tempted to buy all new fabrics. To avoid unnecessary expense, examine any oddments you do have first and use them as a basis for a design, perhaps supplementing them with new fabrics as needed. However, don't take the thrift drive too far and never use areas of worn fabric or mix pure fibres with synthetics if you want your work to last.

Not all fabrics are suitable for patchwork. Choose fabrics of a medium density, that is, with an even weave. Loosely woven fabrics, such as muslin, are not suitable as they are weak and prone to distortion. Very tightly woven fabrics, such as ticking, are not flexible and are therefore difficult to stitch. Stretch fabrics will also distort when stitched.

Cotton is the traditional patchwork fabric and inexperienced needleworkers should use 100% cotton as it is both easy to work with and hard-wearing. With more experience, silk, textured and transparent fabrics, plastics or lightweight wool can be used too for variety.

Sort your oddments into fabric types and weights before selecting, and to begin with only use the same type or weight of fabric in the one piece. If you are using an unusual fabric for the first time, or want to use different types of fabric together, experiment with a small test piece first to gauge the effects.

The same rules can be applied when selecting fabrics for quilting. However, you can be much more experimental with appliqué fabrics as they are stabilized when applied to the ground fabric. This means that textured fabrics can be mixed with plain-weave ones, and light weights may be combined with heavier weights, although the ground should always be the heaviest fabric.

Always pre-wash fabrics in a mild detergent and warm water before starting

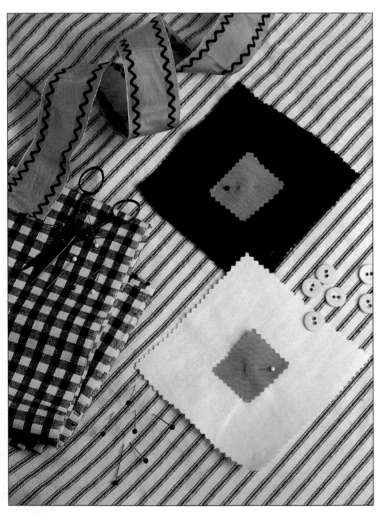

ABOVE: Mid-tone fabric – in this case green – looks dark when contrasted with a light fabric and light when contrasted with a dark one.

ABOVE: Monochromatic colour schemes, where fabrics of the same basic colour in different shades and tones are used together, are more effective when combined with black and white.

work. Wash fabrics that may run separately. When dry, press with a steam iron or with a dry iron and a clean, damp cloth.

TONE AND COLOUR
• • • • • •

Both the colour and tone of a fabric will influence the overall effect of the patterning and therefore the success of your patchwork. Using tone to create depth and interest in an overall design is more effective than using colour alone. Even three-dimensional optical effects can be achieved by carefully using tone to define shape. This will unite a design and create a pattern in what might otherwise be a random and uninteresting work.

Sort your fabrics into three tonal values – light, medium and dark. To identify the value of fabrics, simply examine them through half-closed eyes. When different toned fabrics are arranged together, you will notice that dark tones will appear to recede, while lighter tones stand out. Mid-tone fabrics will look dark when contrasted with light fabrics, but light when placed against dark ones.

Good planning is the most important stage in making a successful piece of work. To begin with, make up test patches and experiment with the positioning of different fabrics to gauge the varied effects you can achieve. With more experience, draw out a scaled-down version of the basic pattern, photocopy it several times, then shade in each shape with coloured pencils to define colour and tone, accentuating different elements on each plan.

COLOUR
• • • • • •

Many patchworkers play safe when organizing a colour scheme, using fabric of the same colour in different tones. This is known as a monochromatic scheme. The method can be made more interesting if the basic colour is combined with black and white. For more adventurous colour schemes, consider the colour wheel. The three primary colours red, blue and yellow are placed opposite the secondary colours green, orange and purple, respectively. The maximum colour contrast occurs between a primary colour and its complementary secondary colour – red and green, blue and orange, and yellow

ABOVE: Here, yellow and purple fabrics in various shades and patterns illustrate the strong colour contrast offered by mixing a primary colour (yellow) with its complementary secondary colour (purple).

and purple. Using complementary colours in either their saturated forms or shades of the colours produces a rich scheme. Conversely, colour harmony may be achieved by using hues closely positioned on the colour wheel, for example the warm shades of red, orange and yellow, or the cool shades of green, blue and purple.

The appearance of colour is greatly effected by the colour that surrounds it. A pale-coloured fabric will appear saturated when placed with a complementary colour. Use white with a mid- or dark-toned colour and it will look bold and strong; use black and the colour will glow.

Repeated use of the same colour in certain parts of the design can create focal points or accents, round which the rest of the design revolves. Traditionally, a red fabric was used at the centre of a Log Cabin patchwork. Brightly coloured fabrics, carefully positioned in a patchwork with the patches cut in the same shape, can also pick out a pattern.

TEXTURED AND PATTERNED FABRIC

Patchworks made up from fabrics of the same or various shades of one colour, but of contrasting textures, will create subtle yet beautiful effects. Use fabrics with a nap (a cut pile which lies in one direction), such as velvet, or fabrics with a distinctive sheen, such as taffeta, to add drama. Colours change subtly as light is reflected off the surface in different ways. Using printed fabric is difficult to do well, but will lend a nostalgic air to patchwork. For an interesting and varied composition, choose a combination of large, medium and small scale prints. Remember that tone is the most important element in the design, so check each print for its value. With a large scale print, select an interesting area from which to cut your patch, such as the centre of a flower or a bud. Use a window template (see Basic Techniques), so you can see the selected area. If you are going to be selective, you will require more fabric.

With spaced motifs, dots or stripes, take time to place the templates. Experiment before you sew, positioning and assembling the shapes to give different results. Bend the rules with striped fabrics. Although in theory is it better to cut on the grain, try cutting some patches on the cross so that the stripes run diagonally. You could then arrange the square so that the stripes radiate out from a centre point or form chevrons.

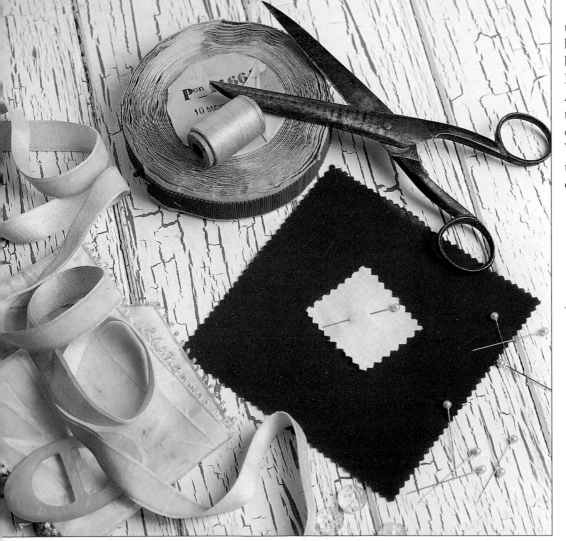

ABOVE LEFT: A more muted colour scheme is provided by choosing fabrics with similar hues. Here warm shades of pink and red provide colour harmony.

LEFT: A pale colour teamed with a mid- or dark-toned colour provides a bold, strong contrast.

OPPOSITE: Colour harmony is provided here, too, using cool shades of green and blue.

BASIC TECHNIQUES

· · · · · ·

The many varied projects in this book feature a wealth of design ideas employing a wide range of techniques, both old and modern, and from all four corners of the world. You will discover the secrets of San Blas appliqué, Seminole patchwork and sashiko quilting, along with shadow work, broderie perse and much more. However, there are many standard quilting, patchwork and appliqué techniques that need to be grasped before you begin a project – you will be coming across the same methods again and again.

PATCHWORK TECHNIQUES

Pieced patchwork is made from fabric scraps which are cut into regular shapes and then sewn together in geometric patterns to form a mosaic of cloth. The patches can be pieced or joined together by one of two basic methods: by machine or by hand. Machining is quickest, but hand sewing gives a traditional look to a finished piece with slightly irregular seams. For the beginner, working over backing papers is the best way to make precise angled shapes when piecing by hand. Whichever method is chosen, accurate templates, meticulous measuring and cutting, careful stitching and thorough pressing are all vital for a professional finish.

TEMPLATES

Accurate templates will allow you to make patches identical in size and shape that will fit perfectly together. There are several different types of template you can make or buy. You can cut them yourself from card (cardboard) or from firm, clear plastic (acetate). Alternatively, you can make window templates, which allow you to view the fabric. Always make a new template for each shape required in a project – old templates eventually become a little distorted round the edges. Templates can also be purchased ready-made in various shapes and sizes.

Patchwork templates should always include a seam allowance; in this book the seam allowance is usually 5 mm (¼ in). If you are using backing papers, you will need to cut two templates if using card or plastic – one with the seam allowance included for marking the fabric and one without the seam allowance for the backing paper. If using a window template, the outside edge of the frame is used to mark the fabric and the inside edge of the frame the backing paper.

MAKING CARD (CARDBOARD) TEMPLATES

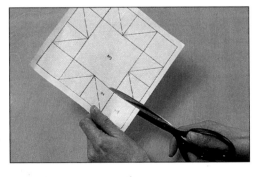

<u>1</u>

Transfer the design on to squared paper and cut round each shape with a sharp pair of scissors.

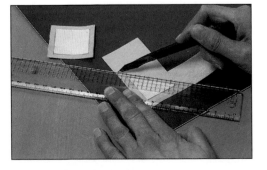

<u>2</u>

Glue the shapes to a piece of thin card (cardboard), and draw a seam allowance round each. Cut out the card.

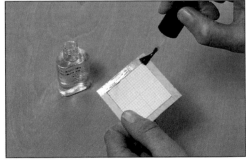

<u>3</u>

Protect the seam allowance area with a thin coat of clear nail varnish.

PREPARING PATCHES

MAKING PLASTIC (ACETATE) TEMPLATES

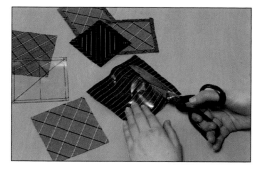

Place the clear plastic (acetate) over the design and draw round each shape. Then draw a seam allowance round each and cut out. Being transparent, the template can be accurately positioned on the fabric.

MAKING WINDOW TEMPLATES

Trace the shape on to card (cardboard), then draw a 5 mm (¼ in) seam allowance round it. Cut out the outer and inner parts, leaving a card frame the exact width of the seam allowance.

MAKING CURVED TEMPLATES

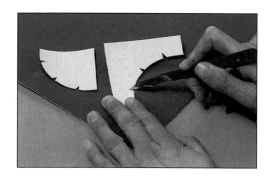

For curved blocks, mark notches on the seam lines of the pattern before cutting it into sections. Cut out each template and then carefully cut out the notches with a craft knife.

Position the template on the fabric, lining up one straight edge with the grain of the fabric. Draw round it on to the reverse of the fabric using a vanishing marker, tailor's chalk or a soft pencil. Butt the shapes together to ensure a good fit.

CUTTING OUT PATCHES IN GROUPS

1

Several patches can be cut at once using this method. Fold the fabric like a concertina and then staple the card (cardboard) template to the layers.

2

Use a sharp rotary cutter or a craft knife and press hard into the cutting mat.

3

Organize the cut pieces by stringing them on a length of thread. You can store them like this and remove them one at a time.

ATTACHING BACKING PAPERS

Pin the backing papers to the reverse of the fabric patches. Fold over or press the seam allowance. Leaving a short free end of thread, tack (baste) along the middle of the seam allowance to the end of the side and trim the corners. Fold over the adjacent seam allowance and continue to tack. Repeat on all sides, leaving the thread ends free so that the threads and the backing papers can be removed easily once the work has been pieced.

BACKING WITH INTERFACING

Iron-on interfacing can be used instead of backing papers. It is especially useful when machine piecing. Mark the patches on the interfacing adjacent to one another. Cut along the main lines first and then cut out the individual blocks. Iron these on to the reverse of the fabric, then mark a seam allowance round the interfacing on the fabric. Cut out the patches individually with scissors or as a group with a rotary cutter.

PIECING OR JOINING PATCHES

Lay out the cut patches to work out the final arrangement. When you are happy with the design, you can begin piecing the patches. There are several different methods of doing this, depending on whether you are piecing by hand or using a sewing machine.

HAND PIECING

Right sides facing, pin the prepared patches together. First pin each corner, and then pin at equidistant points along the side. Join the patches with a small, neat whip stitch – or overstitch – as shown. Insert the needle in one corner and work across to the other, removing the pins as you go.

MACHINE PIECING PATCHES BY THE FLAG METHOD

The flag method enables you to join several pairs of patches in one go. Right sides facing, pin the patches in pairs. Stitch along the seam line using the presser foot as a guide, removing the pins as you go. Leave a short uncut thread between each pair. Remove the flags and cut into units. Join enough pairs to make up the patched piece. To avoid bulk, always press the patch seams flat to one side and not open as in dressmaking.

JOINING PATCHES INTO ROWS

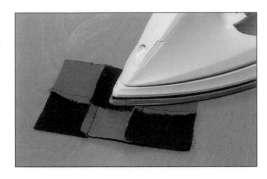

For both hand and machine piecing, make sure that the seam allowances match up perfectly before you pin and stitch the rows together. Press the seams in opposite directions to reduce bulk.

SETTING-IN — BOX PATCHWORK

Setting-in is the term used when a patch is sewn into an angle. To make the angled piece, stitch two pieces together along the seam line, stop stitching 5mm (¼ in) from the end of the seam, and secure with back stitch. Right sides facing, pin one angled piece to the edge of the patch. Stitch from the corner out to the edge, then swing the adjacent angled piece to the other side of the patch, again stitching from the corner out. Press the two seam allowances of the set-in patch toward the angled piece.

SASHING AND BORDERS

These are two very different things although they are cut and sewn in the same way. Sashings are fabric strips used within a design to separate individual patches, or blocks of patches. Borders go round the edges of the work to cover and hide any raw edges.

BLOCKED BORDERS

For the long sides of a border, cut the strips the same length as the quilt. For the short sides, cut the strips the width of the quilt plus the double width of the border. Right sides facing, sew the long strips to the piece first, and then the short strips. Press the seam allowance away from the direction of quilting.

BORDERS WITH MITRED CORNERS

Cut the border strips as above, adding an extra 5 cm (2 in) to all four for mitring, and stitch to the quilt in the usual way. To mitre a corner by hand, press a border strip down at a 45 degree angle, pin and slip stitch on the right side to secure in place. To mitre by machine, work from the wrong side, pressing all the corners back at a 45 degree angle. Pin together and stitch along the fold. Trim the seam allowance and press flat.

LOG CABIN PATCHWORK

Always work from the middle out. Starting with a central square, pin and stitch strips to the square one by one, trimming each strip to the centre as you go. Work round the block anti-clockwise – each new strip will be slightly longer than the previous one. Continue adding strips until you reach the required size. Edge with mitred borders. Often several Log Cabin blocks are made and then stitched together to make a quilt.

QUILTING TECHNIQUES

Quilts are made from three layers: a top piece which is decorated, a layer of wadding (batting) for warmth and a backing piece. These layers are held together with lines of stitching which can be worked in a grid, straight rows or elaborate patterns. Quilted borders, medallions, knots and detailed corners are all possible. Originally, lines of tiny running stitches were worked to offer more warmth. Modern technology and new fibres have made this unnecessary, although the stitches still need to be of equal length.

TACKING (BASTING) QUILTS

Sandwich the wadding (batting) between the top piece and the backing, with the fabrics right side out. Tack (baste) together securely. Knot a long length of thread in a contrasting colour. Work from the middle out, tacking the layers together horizontally, vertically and diagonally. If quilting by machine or with a hoop, add extra lines round the edges.

HAND QUILTING

Place the inner hoop on a flat surface, lay the tacked fabric on top. Place the outer hoop over both and screw the nut to tighten the hoop. Stitch from the top, using your free hand to guide the needle up and down through the layers below.

MACHINE QUILTING

For quilting grids and straight lines, a quilting foot will allow the machine to move more easily over thick fabrics. For free-form quilting, remove the foot and lower the foot lever. Stretch the fabric taut either with a hoop or your hands, and stitch slowly so that you can accurately guide the stitches.

APPLIQUÉ TECHNIQUES

Appliqué can be worked in a variety of fabrics, including silk, wool and cotton, and strong, closely woven fabric is possibly the best choice. Felt is popular for appliqué designs because it does not fray. Design ideas are limitless and virtually any shape can be used. Broderie perse, Hawaiian appliqué and stained glass appliqué, together with cut and sew, inlaid and reverse appliqué methods, are just a few of the techniques featured in the book.

IRON-ON FUSIBLE BONDING WEB

  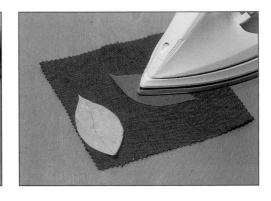

<u>1</u>

A quick and easy way to attach appliqué to the fabric. Because the appliqué fabric is fused to the web, it won't fray. Trace the outline on to the fusible web.

<u>2</u>

Roughly cut out the design and iron this on to the fabric. Cut round the outline with a sharp pair of scissors, a rotary cutter or craft knife.

<u>3</u>

Peel off the backing paper and iron, fusing the motif to the main fabric. Set the machine to a zig zag and stitch round the raw edge of the motif.

PIN TACKING (BASTING)

BELOW: This simple appliqué sunflower has been stitched on by hand.

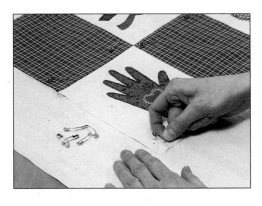

Tack (baste) the seam allowance round the appliqué design. Mark the placement lines on the right side of the fabric. Arrange the appliqué shapes on the fabric following these lines. First position the background pieces, and then layer any extra pieces on top. Alternatively, attach the pieces with double-sided tape.

STITCHES
· · · · · ·

Straight stitch is the standard machine sewing stitch, worked in straight lines and secured by back stitch at the end of each seam. Machine tacking stitches are worked by setting the machine to the longest stitch. To attach appliqué and crazy patchwork, set the machine to a close zig zag stitch and work a row of satin stitches. The following hand stitches are used throughout the book.

RUNNING STITCH

This is the main stitch used for hand quilting. It is also used for sewing seams in patchwork and quilting. Stitches should be of an even length, no bigger than 3 mm (⅛ in), and can be run a few at a time. Running stitch is also used in sashiko and kantha work.

HOLBEIN STITCH

Work a row of running stitch in one direction and then fill in the spaces on the return journey.

SLIP-STITCH

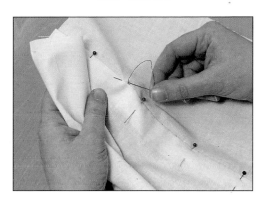

This stitch is used to secure a finished edge to another surface, like an appliqué or a binding. With the needle, catch a thread under the fabric together with a single thread on the fold of the fabric, spacing these small stitches evenly apart.

WHIP STITCH

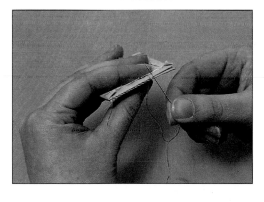

Also known as oversewing and overcasting, this small straight stitch is used to hold together two edges. Work from back to front, inserting the needle at an angle and picking up a thread from each piece at the same time.

STAB STITCH

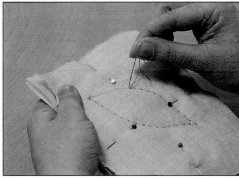

This stitch replaces running stitch when quilting thick fabric. Hold the needle perpendicular to the fabric, and work one stitch at a time. It is also used to outline individual shapes on quilted fabric.

BLANKET STITCH

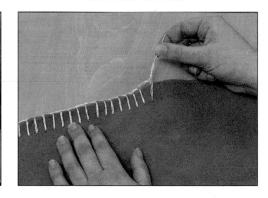

Blanket, or buttonhole, stitch is ideal for finishing off raw or scalloped edges on fabrics that don't fray, such as felt or blanket. It can also be worked over a fold. Insert the needle into the back so that it points up to the raw edge, wind the loose thread over the needle and pull through the loop. Make a decorative feature of large blanket stitches by sewing them in a contrasting colour.

GENERAL TECHNIQUES
· · · · · ·

FINDING THE GRAIN OF THE FABRIC

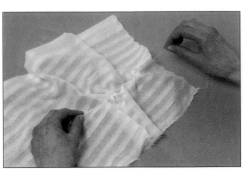

It is necessary to find the grain to straighten raw edges. Nick the fabric just below the raw edge, pull a thread gently across the fabric and cut along the line made. You can pull threads to fringe a piece of fabric and also to mark a grid. Sometimes you will need to find the straight grain in order to centre a motif.

ENLARGING A DESIGN

Trace the motif on to squared paper. On another sheet of paper, mark out the same number of squares to the required size of the finished design. Copy the motif on to the new grid so that the lines of the design correspond exactly with the original.

TRANSFERRING A DESIGN ON TO FABRIC

1

Copy the design on to dressmaker's carbon paper. Place the carbon on the reverse of the fabric and then trace over the outline with a pen, pressing heavily.

2

Pouncing is used to transfer a design on to the right side of the fabric for an appliqué or quilting design. Trace over the design on to paper with a dressmaker's wheel or an unthreaded sewing machine, so that the design appears as a broken line. Push tailor's chalk through the pierced paper with a brush or sponge to mark the fabric.

3

Trace the design on to tissue paper, pin to the wrong side of the fabric then machine round the outline. Rip away the tissue paper to reveal the outline. This method is good for fine or fragile fabric.

BELOW: This drawstring bag shows designs transferred on to the patchwork squares.

MAKING AND USING BIAS STRIPS

Bias strips are used for binding, piping and also in the stained glass appliqué method. Cut a square on the straight grain, fold it in half diagonally and stitch together the open edges. Press the seam allowance flat and trim. Mark parallel lines on to the fabric and then roll it into a tube so that the top edge aligns with the first marked line. Pin and stitch along this line. Press the seam flat and trim. Cut along the marked lines into one long continuous strip of bias binding. Alternatively, cut several strips on the diagonal and then join them together, pressing the seam allowance flat.

BINDING A MITRED CORNER

<u>1</u>

Stitch along one edge, reducing the size of the stitches near the corner. Stop stitching 5 mm (¼ in) from the corner, lift the presser foot and swivel the quilt to stitch the next edge. A tuck will form in the binding at the corner. Lower the presser foot, and carry on stitching the next side.

<u>2</u>

Fold over the binding, pin and sew close to the previous stitching line. Fold the tuck diagonally to mitre the corners and slip-stitch in place.

ENVELOPE CUSHION COVER

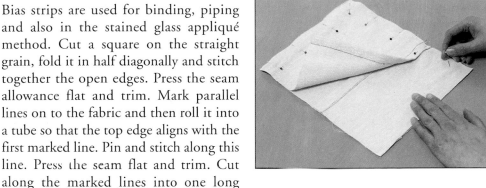

For the front, cut a square to fit the cushion pad, adding 1 cm (½ in) seam allowance on all sides. Cut a back piece 2.5 cm (1 in) bigger on one side, and then cut in half lengthways. Press, and sew a 1 cm (½ in) hem along the cut edge of both back pieces. Right sides facing, pin the front to the back pieces so that one hem lies slightly over the other. Sew round all four seams and, if directed, stitch in piping or fringing now. Clip the corners, press and turn right side out.

STRETCHING AND MOUNTING A PICTURE

Stretch the finished piece taut over the backing. Using a strong thread, stitch back and forth, joining the raw edges in a criss cross pattern and pulling the thread tightly as you go. Work the long sides first, then repeat with the short sides. Secure to the backing board with tape.

DRAWSTRING BAG

<u>1</u>

Pin together two rectangles in main fabric and sew round three sides, leaving the top short side open. Cut two rectangles the same size in lining and stitch the two long sides. Stitch part way across the short end, break off for 5 cm (2 in), then stitch to the end. Right sides facing, pin the two bags together and stitch a continuous line round the top edge. Trim and clip the seam. Pull the bag through the lining. Press and slip-stitch to close the gap.

<u>2</u>

Push the lining into the bag and press flat. For the channel, machine stitch two parallel lines, 1 cm (½ in) from the top edge and 1 cm (½ in) apart. Make a hole in the seam between the two rows of stitching with a stitch unpicker and thread the drawstring through.

· · · · · ·

HISTORIC STYLE

· · · · · ·

Patchwork, appliqué and quilting have a fascinating past which reflects the social history of the time. The cotton patchwork quilts made by the early American settlers are quite different to the richly decorated crazy patchwork loved by the Victorians. Recreate the historical style by stitching one of these beautiful traditional designs, perhaps to commemorate a wedding or birth and create your own family heirloom.

INTRODUCTION

ABOVE: This design is based on a sampler quilt made in Pennsylvannia, in about 1870.

BELOW: A late 19th-century Welsh quilt.

Patchwork, quilting and appliqué have developed over the centuries in many different countries. Techniques have crossed continents, fallen in and out of fashion, and evolved according to cultural and economic changes.

Originally these crafts were practised through necessity, rather than pleasure. Patchwork was an economic way of using scraps for those who could not afford new fabric; appliqué was used to replace worn areas on a textile; and quilting provided vital warmth. However, many historic examples show that both professional and domestic makers combined function with decoration. Patchwork developed intricate patterns known as mosaic patchwork, made of hundreds of tiny geometric shapes pieced together. This was a time-consuming method of construction, with traditional hand-sewn pieces of cloth backed with paper. Closer examination of these papers reveals part of the makers' lives as templates were often cut from old letters, newspapers or magazines. It is sometimes possible to date the pieces, or to show that a quilt had proved to be too ambitious for the original maker, only to be unearthed years later and completed by another member of the family.

People often re-used fabric scraps which were simply too valuable to throw away. In the Victorian era, a fashion emerged for using rich and opulent fabrics in the randomly arranged crazy patchwork, in contrast to patchwork's humble and utilitarian beginnings. Patchwork also became a vehicle for practising stitches, and a way to express personal messages and sentimental phrases. Work was embellished with elaborate embroidery stitches and motifs, ribbons and buttons, so that the whole textile was imbued with memories. These amazingly decorative quilts provided a canvas on which a needlewoman could display her skills.

Quilts have always been associated with the celebration of important events. Typically they would be made to mark a particular occasion, with the nature of the celebration reflected in the choice of design or quilting. The Double Wedding Ring patchwork design, for example, was worked to mark a marriage or wedding anniversary and was made from interlinking rings, each constructed from tiny patches. It would be inadvisable to attempt an entire quilt with this motif today, because it is so time consuming. Appearances are deceptive, however. The Cathedral Window patchwork design, which looks complicated, is in fact relatively easy to construct and is more an exercise in fabric origami as the patches consist of folded and re-folded cloth.

In the early stages of its history, quilting was considered simply as a utilitarian technique. Two layers of fabric were placed either side of a filling of wadding (batting). The three layers were then stitched together to create a flexible and insulating textile. Although these basic skills fulfilled the practical necessity of providing a warm bedcover, people quickly recognized the decorative potential of quilting to create interesting relief patterns. Trapunto, or stuffed, quilting and corded, or Italian, quilting are two such techniques, which were not used for their insulating qualities but became popular for embellishing clothing. In corded quilting, two layers of fabric are placed together on top of a loosely woven

LEFT: A naive and charming example of the decorative crazy quilt that was popular in the latter half of the 19th century.

underpiece and a pattern of narrow channels are stitched. Cord is then threaded through from the wrong side to create relief pattern. This method is often used in conjunction with traditional quilting to outline a motif, or to delineate an area. Trapunto quilting is constructed in much the same way, but instead of channels shapes are stitched and filled with wadding from the wrong side. Shadow quilting, another historic technique, uses a sheer fabric as a top layer over coloured wool or cord to create subtle areas of diffused colour. Traditionally made in white fabrics, it can also be effective in other colours.

Appliqué originated in the early spirit of "make do and mend", and developed along decorative and creative lines. The technique of broderie perse was practised during the 18th and 19th centuries to preserve favourite motifs from imported Indian cotton chintzes. These offered a strong contrast to Western fabrics, featuring bold, brilliant designs with large birds, cornucopias and flowers. Such was their popularity that British manufacturers suffered a loss of trade and a law was passed first to limit their importation and finally to ban their use. Unable to replenish their stocks, needlewomen cut out the motifs to appliqué on to other fabrics.

Inspired by historical examples of patchwork, quilting and appliqué, these step-by-step projects are guaranteed to give pleasure to the maker. They have been devised to encourage the amateur needleworker to attempt traditional methods, and although challenging, the projects are not so large or complex as to discourage the beginner. It is advisable to start small and simple – projects such as lavender bags, nightdress cases and bootees are ideal for beginners. To help re-create the romance of the past, choose evocative fabrics, such as velvets, satins, taffetas and brocades. Do not forget trimmings, search out unusual beads, ribbons, fringing and tassels to add to your collection.

BELOW: This intricate modern quilt is based on the Baltimore quilt designs, popular in the 19th century.

VELVET SCARF

Squares arranged on the diagonal form the serrated edge to the patchwork borders on this wide scarf.
The patches are cut from both silk and velvet to create an interesting texture.

YOU WILL NEED
· · · · · ·

*thin card (cardboard)
and pencil*

craft knife

dressmaker's scissors

*scraps of silk and velvet in
pink, rust and brown*

*1 m x 90 cm
(1 yd x 36 in) velvet*

*sewing machine and
matching thread*

iron

dressmaker's pins

*1.8 m x 40 cm
(72 in x 16 in) silk lining*

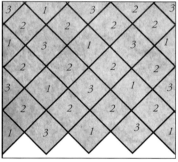

PREPARATION

Follow the plan below. Each border uses 26 squares. Make the templates 9 cm (3½ in) square. Cut out 24 rust squares, 14 pink squares, 14 brown (velvet and silk) squares. Halve three of the pink squares and cut one diagonally into quarters. Halve six of the brown squares. Follow the plan and arrange the patches in two borders. Cut the velvet widthways and sew into a piece 2 m (2 yd) long.

KEY: 1 = BROWN
2 = RUST
3 = PINK

1
Sew the squares into strips and then join the strips into one piece (see Basic Techniques). Insert the triangles in the sides and top to make three straight edges. Press the seams. Make the second border.

2
Measure the borders and trim the velvet to fit. Pin the straight edge of each border to the velvet. Machine stitch close to the edge and then appliqué with a zig zag stitch. Trim and press.

3
Right sides facing, pin the velvet piece to the silk lining. Stitch round the seams leaving a gap on one long edge. Trim and clip the corners. Turn right side out and press. Slipstitch the opening.

VELVET SLIPPERS

These children's slippers are made from velvet and silk scraps. The tops have been quilted with tiny kantha stitches. These repetitive filling stitches can run in any direction and are commonly worked on Indian kantha quilts.

YOU WILL NEED

dressmaker's paper and pencil

dressmaker's scissors

30 cm x 90 cm
(12 in x 36 in) velvet

30 cm x 90 cm
(12 in x 36 in) silk

15 cm x 90 cm
(6 in x 36 in) calico

needle and tacking
(basting) thread

craft knife

pair of insoles

fabric marker

fabric glue

metallic thread

sewing machine and
matching thread

dressmaker's pins

pair of soles

4 small tassels

PREPARATION

Enlarge and draw the templates on to paper and cut out four slipper tops in both velvet and silk. Cut out four calico lining pieces and tack (baste) these to the reverse of the velvet. Cut a pair of insoles to size. Trace round the insoles on to a piece of velvet, adding a seam allowance and cut out.

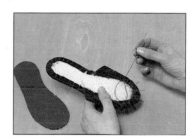

1

Place the insoles on the reverse of the velvet. Clip the seam allowance and turn under. Glue the edges, pressing firmly in place.

2

Decorate the velvet tops with metallic thread using tiny running stitches (see Basic Techniques). Join the tops along the centre seam. Right sides facing, stitch the velvet to the silk lining along the front edge. Turn right side out and tack (baste) the raw edges.

3

Pin the tops to the insoles and secure with slip-stitch.

TO FINISH

Glue the soles to the base of the slippers, hiding the turnings. Leave to dry. Sew the tassels to the slipper tops.

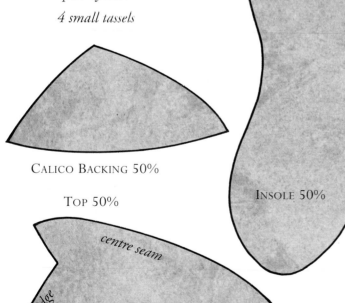

CALICO BACKING 50%

TOP 50%

INSOLE 50%

centre seam

front edge

CRAZY PATCHWORK CUSHION

The appliqué on this cushion looks like crazy paving. The irregularly shaped patches are arranged at random. Choose fabrics of a similar texture and with varying tonal values for a professional look.

YOU WILL NEED
• • • • •

dressmaker's scissors

60 cm x 90 cm (24 in x 36 in) cotton fabric

thin card (cardboard) and pencil

scraps of fabric in six contrasting patterns

dressmaker's pins

needle and tacking (basting) thread

matching thread

iron

1.8 m (72 in) cotton furnishing (upholstery) fringe

sewing machine

38 cm (15 in) zip (zipper)

46 cm (18 in) square cushion pad

PREPARATION

Cut the cotton fabric into two 46 cm (18 in) squares. Enlarge the diagram and cut card (cardboard) templates to cover one square. A rough, open-textured cotton was used for the base, complemented with patches cut from scraps of furnishing fabrics with interesting, open weaves.

TO FINISH

Press the squares flat and, right sides facing, pin the fringe to one square. Stitch into the seams as you make up the cover. Insert the zip (zipper). Insert the cushion pad.

1

Cut out the crazy patches from the scraps of fabric, adding a 5 mm (¼ in) turning all round.

2

Tack (baste) the templates to the scraps. Pin and tack to the cushion fabric.

3

Slip-stitch round each shape in matching thread, to secure to the base.

DIAGRAM OF WHOLE COVER 33⅓%

HATPIN CUSHION

An appliqué of crazy patchwork, in velvet, satin and silk, has been stitched into an extra large pin cushion for storing decorative hatpins.

YOU WILL NEED

dressmaker's scissors

dressmaker's paper

pair of compasses and pencil

scraps of silk, velvet and satin

50 cm x 90 cm
(20 in x 36 in) calico

dressmaker's pins

sewing machine and
matching threads

iron

wadding (batting)

needle

PREPARATION

Cut out the templates in paper. You will need a circular template with a diameter of 18 cm (7 in) for the base/top, and a rectangular one measuring 52 cm x 10 cm (20½ in x 4 in) for the band. Cut a silk base, and one top and one band in calico. Cut a strip on the bias in both velvet and silk measuring 52 cm x 5 cm (20½ in x 2 in).

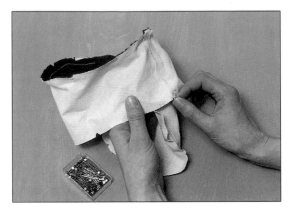

1

Join the short ends of the calico band together and stitch the band to the silk base. Pin and stitch the calico top to the calico band leaving a small gap to turn through. Trim, press and fill with wadding (batting). Stitch the gap closed.

2

Cut out lots of random patches from the scraps. Turn under the raw edges and machine stitch the patches together, laying them over each other to make a piece of crazy patchwork. Cut out a top, using the template. Make a narrow patched strip from silk and velvet squares 52 cm (20½ in) long. Position the velvet and silk bias strips side by side and place the patched strip over the join. Pin, turn the raw edges under and machine stitch.

3

With right sides together, stitch the patched band to the patched top. Press and turn right side out.

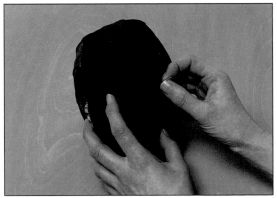

4

Pull the outer patched cover over the inner pad, turn a hem and slip-stitch along the edge.

SQUARE LINEN QUILT

This *faux* antique, square quilt is made up in white linen. The quilt is knotted in perlé thread in an even grid pattern, and stitches run round the borders in three lines to complement the look.

YOU WILL NEED
• • • • • •

vanishing marker

90 cm (36 in) square
white linen

ruler

dressmaker's pins

needle and tacking
(basting) thread

90 cm (36 in) square
wadding (batting)

2 skeins navy perlé thread

crewel needle

90 cm (36 in) square calico

matching thread

dressmaker's scissors

<u>1</u>

Using the vanishing marker, mark the linen with a dot at intervals of 5 cm (2 in) down the length. Centre the positioning so that the first dot at top, bottom and side are an equal distance away from the edges of the fabric. Draw out a single thread the width of the fabric at each point (see Basic Techniques).

<u>2</u>

Turn the fabric to the wrong side and measure along the pulled lines every 5 cm (2 in) and mark a dot with the vanishing marker. Turn over again.

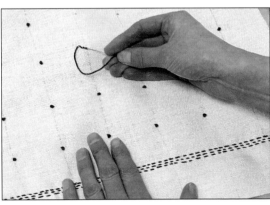

<u>3</u>

Tack (baste) the linen to the wadding (batting). Using the perlé thread, make a French knot over each dot, starting in the centre and working out. Run three parallel lines of running stitch, just outside the first dots marked, to edge the quilt.

TO FINISH

Pin the calico backing to the linen, with right sides facing. Machine stitch round the edges, leaving a gap. Turn the quilt right sides out, slip-stitch the opening closed and press. Top stitch round the edges, just inside the decorative border, to hold the wadding (batting) in place.

BATHROOM CURTAINS

These floaty curtains have a shell design appliquéd in delicate shades of pink on to fine voile. The raw edges of the shell are closely covered with buttonhole stitch to prevent them from fraying.

YOU WILL NEED

pair of voile curtains

tracing paper and pen

25 cm x 90 cm
(10 in x 36 in) cream voile

dressmaker's carbon paper

dressmaker's pins

needle and tacking
(basting) thread

embroidery hoop

pale pink perlé thread

crewel needle

embroidery scissors

PREPARATION

Make or buy a pair of voile curtains to fit your windows. Draw a curtain plan to work out where to position the shells and how many you will need. The amount of voile specified is sufficient for six appliqué shells.

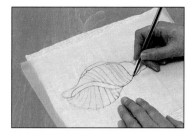

1

Trace the template on to tracing paper. Place over a piece of voile with dressmaker's carbon paper sandwiched in between. Draw over the outlines in pen to transfer the design.

2

Aligning the fabric grain, position and tack (baste) the voile to the right side of the curtain. Place in the hoop and, using perlé thread, work the outlines in tiny buttonhole stitch and the interior lines in a mixture of stem stitch and running stitch (see Basic Techniques).

TO FINISH

Make as many appliqué shells as you need. Using embroidery scissors, carefully trim the excess voile round each shell's outline as close to the stitching as possible.

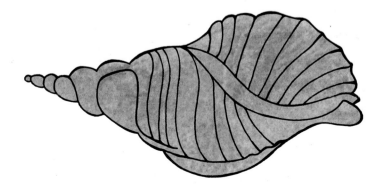

TEAPOT COVER

Stab stitches are worked around the outline of the printed floral motifs to raise and emphasize them on this quilted teapot cover. The teapot sits snuggly inside the closed fabric "box".

YOU WILL NEED
• • • • • •

dressmaker's paper and pencil

dressmaker's scissors

*50 cm x 90 cm
(20 in x 36 in) floral fabric*

*50 cm x 90 cm
(20 in x 36 in)
wadding (batting)*

dressmaker's pins

*needle and tacking
(basting) thread*

matching thread

small piece of Velcro

PREPARATION

Enlarge the templates. Cut four side pieces and two bases in fabric, and two side pieces and one base in wadding (batting), adding 5 mm (¼ in) seam allowances all round.

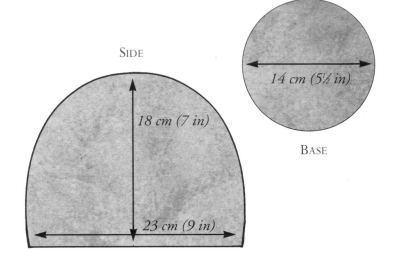

SIDE

18 cm (7 in)

23 cm (9 in)

14 cm (5½ in)

BASE

1
Place two fabric side pieces right sides together and tack (baste) to the wadding (batting). Stitch along the curved edge. Repeat for the other side and for the base. Clip the seams. Press and turn right side out. Top stitch 1 cm (½ in) from the curved edge.

2
Work in stab stitch round the flower shapes so that they stand out in high relief (see Basic Techniques). Outlining the individual motifs in this way quilts the fabric. Turn inside out again.

3
Pin and stitch the sides to the base. Trim and clip the base seam close to the stitching.

TO FINISH

Turn right side out, then tack (baste) and top stitch round the base 1 cm (½ in) from the edge, to enclose the raw edges. Sew on a small piece of Velcro to fasten the top.

POT HOLDER

This pot holder has been inspired by a Charles Rennie Mackintosh design, which can be found on some of the walls of Glasgow School of Art.

YOU WILL NEED

dressmaker's scissors

30 cm (12 in) square mustard fabric

20 cm x 26 cm (8 in x 10 in) pink cotton fabric

22 cm x 24 cm (8½ in x 9½ in) polyester wadding (batting)

26 cm x 28 cm (10 x 11 in) blue and white checked fabric

dressmaker's pins

needle and tacking (basting) thread

iron

matching threads

PREPARATION

Cut four mustard and eight pink 6 cm (2¼ in) squares. Cut a mustard rectangle the same size as the wadding (batting). Centre the wadding on the reverse side of the checked fabric and tack (baste) in position.

1

Press under a small turning on each side of the squares. Pin the small mustard squares to the centre front of the checked fabric. Pin a pink square to each corner and then centre a pink square on each side.

2

Slip-stitch the squares in place. Tack (baste) the mustard rectangle to the back, covering the wadding (batting). Press under a small turning on each side of the checked fabric, then turn again to cover the edges of the wadding and backing fabric. Slip-stitch in place and mitre the corners (see Basic Techniques). Sew a pink fabric loop to the centre of one edge, for hanging.

CATHEDRAL WINDOW NEEDLECASE

Don't be frightened if this piece of patchwork looks complicated. It is in fact easy to construct. This is not really a quilting method, but because the patches are layered the resulting fabric is very warm and so the idea could be translated into a quilt.

YOU WILL NEED

scrap of taffeta

dressmaker's scissors

iron

dressmaker's pins

needle and matching thread

scrap of silk organza

scrap of lining fabric

sewing machine and matching thread

4 pieces of felt

pinking shears

button

PREPARATION

Cut eight squares of taffeta on the straight grain, twice the intended size of the patch. Press under the raw edges.

1

Find the centre point of each square by matching opposite corners and press on the fold.

2

Fold each corner to the centre point. Press and pin in place.

3

Fold each corner to the centre point once more, then press and pin. Secure the corners at the centre with one small stitch.

4

Place two patches, wrong sides facing and whip stitch across the top. Sew two rows of four blocks in this way, and then join the rows.

5

Measure the fold from one corner to the centre point of one patch. Cut ten squares to this size in silk organza. Pin each piece diagonally over the seam. To cover the raw edge of the organza, roll the fold over and slip-stitch in place. Do the same on all the folds to create the cathedral window effect.

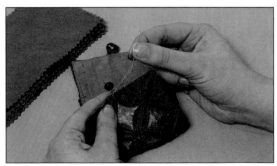

6

Cut the lining fabric to fit the case, adding a 5 mm (¼ in) seam allowance. Press under the seam allowance. Wrong sides facing, slip-stitch the lining to the needlecase. Sew a button on one side and a fabric loop on the other. Cut the felt to size and pink the edges. Stack the felt pieces, place in the needlecase and stitch down the centre line.

FOLDED-STAR PIN CUSHION

Although deceptively intricate, this pin cushion is easy to make. Squares are folded into triangles and then arranged on the base to make the star. Because the patches are unfitted and without seams, this technique is not classed as a true patchwork.

YOU WILL NEED

scraps of taffeta in two colours
dressmaker's scissors
iron
scrap of cotton fabric
dressmaker's pins
needle and matching threads
pair of compasses and pencil
scrap of velvet
sewing machine
stuffing

PREPARATION

Cut 12 taffeta rectangles 5 cm x 9 cm (2 in x 3½ in) in colour one, and eight the same size in colour two. Press a 5 mm (¼ in) turning along one long side of each rectangle. Cut a cotton base, 20 cm (8 in) square. Fold the opposite corners, first lengthways and then widthways into the centre of the square. Press along the fold lines.

1

On each rectangular patch, fold the two corners on the turned side down to the centre to form a triangle, and press.

2

Arrange four triangles in colour one on the centre of the base fabric, with folded sides facing, to form a square. Pin and slip-stitch the folded edges to the base.

3

For the second layer, arrange eight triangles in colour two round the centre point. First, pin four triangles to the base 2 cm (¾ in) from the centre, with the folded sides running parallel to the square. Then pin four diagonally so that they overlap these. Slip-stitch the outer edges.

4

Arrange eight triangles in colour one. Pin each triangle to the base, overlapping the previous layer, positioned 4 cm (1½ in) from the centre. Slip-stitch the triangle points to the base and tack (baste) round the outer edges.

TO FINISH

With the compass point centred, draw a circle round the star close to the outside edge. Cut a matching circle in velvet. Right sides facing, stitch the star to the velvet. Leave a small gap to turn through. Clip and press. Turn right side out. Fill with stuffing and slip-stitch the gap.

PATCHWORK BEAR

Soft toys, like this delightful satin bear, were often made from patchwork in days gone by. Colourful satin patches are pieced together in box patchwork and then cut into a bear shape.

YOU WILL NEED
• • • • • •

*thin card (cardboard)
and pencil*

craft knife

*50 cm x 90 cm (20 in x
36 in) iron-on interfacing*

dressmaker's scissors

iron

*scraps of satin fabric in
assorted colours*

dressmaker's pins

*sewing machine and
matching thread*

*needle and tacking
(basting) thread*

rotary cutter

stuffing

PREPARATION

Enlarge and make the teddy template and cut out in card (cardboard). Enlarge and make templates 1 and 2 in card and transfer to the interfacing. Cut enough for two patched pieces for the bear, cutting twice as many patches from 2. Make all of piece 1 in one fabric. Make piece 2 in assorted colours, so that there is an equal number of light and dark shades. Iron the interfacing to the fabric scraps, then cut out the patches with a 5 mm (¼ in) seam allowance. When making up each box, join one light and one dark piece so that the dark piece is always on the same side in order to create the illusion of depth.

1

Right sides facing, join one light and one dark piece 2 to form an angle. Press the seam to one side. Pin piece 1 to the angled patch matching the corners. Stitch from one corner in the middle of the angle to the end of the seam and cut the threads. Swivel the adjacent angled piece to the other edge of piece 1 and pin. Stitch from the centre point to the end of the seam (for setting-in see Basic Techniques).

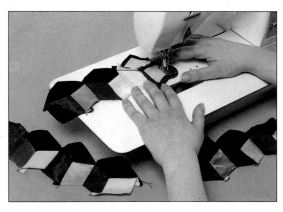

2

Make lots of boxes and stitch them together in horizontal rows. Press the seams in one direction only. Carefully tack (baste) the horizontal rows of box patchwork together and stitch. Press the seams in opposite directions (see Basic Techniques).

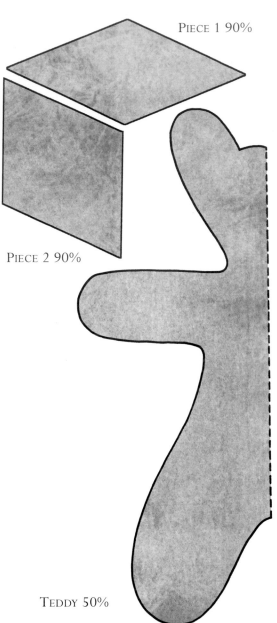

PIECE 1 90%

PIECE 2 90%

TEDDY 50%

TO FINISH

Make two patched pieces large enough for the bear. Cut out two bears without a seam allowance in interfacing. Iron to the wrong side of each patch. Fold the patch in half and pin the template along the fold line, adding a seam allowance. Cut out two pieces the same in box patchwork with a rotary cutter. Right sides facing, starting on an inside leg, stitch round the shape leaving 5 cm (2 in) open. Clip into the corners, trim and press. Turn right side out, fill with stuffing and slip-stitch the gap.

VELVET THROW

This project shows how to make a patched piece of velvet. Pairs of triangles are sewn into diamonds and then grouped into stars. The patchwork could easily be made into a quilt or a cushion.

YOU WILL NEED

thin card (cardboard) and pencil

iron-on interfacing

craft knife

iron

assorted velvet scraps

rotary cutter

dressmaker's pins

sewing machine and matching thread

silk lining fabric

needle and matching thread

PREPARATION

Measure the size required for the patch. Draw a triangle, with a base half the length of the other sides, and transfer on to card (cardboard). Work out how many templates will be needed and cut out in interfacing using a craft knife. Iron to the wrong side of the velvet and cut out the pieces with a 5 mm (¼ in) seam allowance. Arrange the cut triangles and manipulate into diamonds with the best design possibility. Combine the diamonds to make stars, using colour carefully. Draw a plan for reference.

1

Pin and stitch pairs of triangles together along the short edge to form a diamond, using the flag method (see Basic Techniques). Cut joining threads and press the seams flat.

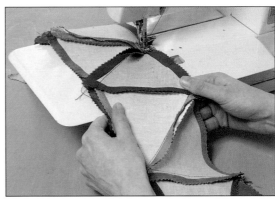

2

Stitch the pairs together in horizontal strips following your own colour scheme, and then join the strips together to make up the finished piece. Press the seams in opposite directions to reduce bulk (see Basic Techniques).

TO FINISH

To make the patched piece into a throw, cut a piece of silk lining to fit. Right sides facing, stitch round the seam line, leaving a 10 cm (4 in) gap. Clip the corners and press. Turn right side out and slip-stitch the opening. To make a quilt or cushion cover, see Basic Techniques for instructions.

SUITING THROW

This gentleman's throw is made out of scraps of suiting fabrics bought from a tailor. The scraps are cut into rectangles so that the stripes and patterns run in as many directions as possible.

YOU WILL NEED

*thin card (cardboard)
and pencil*

craft knife

scraps of suiting

dressmaker's pencil

dressmaker's scissors

dressmaker's pins

*sewing machine and
matching thread*

*silk lining in a
contrasting colour*

needle and matching thread

iron

tacking (basting) thread

shirt buttons

PREPARATION

Cut a rectangular template in card (cardboard) and calculate the number of patches required. Transfer the template to the suiting using a dressmaker's pencil. Cut out the patches with a 5 mm (¼ in) seam allowance. Pin and stitch together in pairs using the flag method (see Basic Techniques). Stitch the pairs in horizontal rows and press the seams.

1
Join the horizontal strips of suiting together to make a large patched piece. Trim the seams and press in opposite directions to reduce bulk (see Basic Techniques).

2
Measure the patch and add 13 cm (5 in) all round for a loose border. Cut the silk lining to this measurement. Right sides facing, pin the lining to the patched piece and stitch 1 cm (½ in) from the edge. Leave a 10 cm (4 in) opening on one side and the corners free. Press the seam and pull through. Slip-stitch the gap.

3
Iron a loose and even fold of silk around the border. Pin and tack (baste) in place.

TO FINISH

Top stitch in matching thread close to the seam line between the suiting and the silk. Mitre the corners and slip-stitch (see Basic Techniques). Sew the shirt buttons round the border, as shown.

LAVENDER BAG

Stars are frequently found in patchwork and the LeMoyne Star is a popular choice. To achieve this tricky eight-seam join that meets in the centre of the star, work slowly and carefully.

YOU WILL NEED

tracing paper and pencil

thin (card) cardboard

craft knife

scraps of silk organza in three colours

rotary cutter

scrap of lining silk

dressmaker's pins

sewing machine and matching thread

needle and matching thread

dried lavender

ribbon

PREPARATION

Trace the star and make the templates. For each star (you will need two), cut out eight pieces from template 1 in two colours and four pieces each from templates 2 and 3 in the third colour. Use a rotary cutter, if wished.

1

To make the star, with right sides facing, pin together two of piece 1, in two colours, and stitch. Make another pair to match. Press flat.

LeMoyne Star

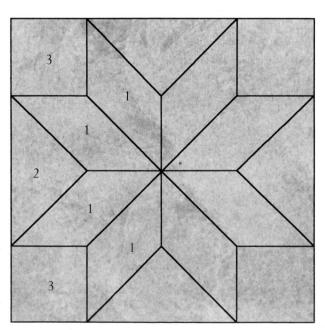

2

Join the two pairs together, carefully matching the centre seams, pin and stitch. Press the seam flat to one side. Make the other half of the star in the same way.

3

To set in the square 3, swivel the square to match the corner points and pin to the angled edge (see Basic Techniques). To set in the triangle 2, match the corner points and pin to the angled edge. Stitch and press.

TO FINISH

Set in three more squares, and three more triangles to make the patch. Make a second patch the same. Measure one side and cut two pieces of organza this length plus 5 cm (2 in) wide. Stitch one to the top of each patch and press. Right sides facing, stitch round the base and sides of the bag and turn through. Fold a 1 cm (½ in) hem round the top of the bag, press and top stitch. Fill the bag with dried lavender and tie with a ribbon bow.

NIGHTDRESS CASE

This patchwork design is traditionally used on quilts to celebrate a marriage. The curved lines meet and overlap at regular intervals, giving the overall impression of two interlocking rings.

YOU WILL NEED
• • • • • •

thin card (cardboard)

craft knife

dressmaker's scissors

scraps of organza in five colours

dressmaker's pins

sewing machine and matching thread

iron

needle and matching thread

press studs (snap fasteners)

PREPARATION

Make the templates from the back of the book. Each wedding ring design is made up of eight arcs, four patches 4 and one centre 5, and you will need six wedding rings in total. For each arc, cut four of section 1 in the first colour. Cut 32 of 1. For each arc, cut two of section 2 in the second colour. Cut 16 of 2. For four arcs only, cut one of section 3 in colour four, and cut one of section 3 in colour five. Cut eight of 3. Cut two of 4 in the second, and two of 4 in the third colour. Cut two of 5 in the fourth, and two of 5 in the fifth colour.

1

To make an arc, pin together and stitch four pieces of section 1. Press seams to one side. Pin and stitch one piece of section 2 at each end of the arc.

3

For the four remaining arcs, pin and stitch section 3 at each end of the arc, in two contrasting colours. Press seams to one side.

5

Take section 5 and match the notch to the centre seam on one of the oval patches, align the corners and stitch. Press the seam towards the oval. Pin the second oval piece to the other curved edge of 5, matching the centre points and alternating the colours of the patches. Stitch and press towards the oval.

2

Take section 4 and match the notch to the centre seam of one arc, and align the end pieces to the points of 2. Pin and stitch. Make three more patches the same.

4

Match the centre seam of one patched arc to the notch on 4. Pin and stitch. Press the seam to the arc. Make four patches in the same way.

TO FINISH

Join a second piece 5 to the curved edge of the second oval as before and continue to make a square. Measure the square, add a 1 cm (½ in) seam allowance on three sides and a 2 cm (¾ in) seam allowance on the other. Cut a piece of organza to fit. Halve the long edge and cut. Press under a double hem on both pieces and stitch. Overlap the two pieces, right sides to the patched piece and make an envelope cover (see Basic Techniques). Make a silk lining in the same way, if wished. Stitch pairs of press studs (snap fasteners) to the opening.

CORDED PURSE

Corded quilting is a very old technique that was popular in Italy and so became known as Italian quilting. The fabric is quilted in parallel lines to make channels, which are then threaded with cord or yarn to form raised lines. This method is often used with trapunto quilting.

YOU WILL NEED
· · · · · ·

tissue paper and marker pen

*30 cm x 90 cm
(12 in x 36 in) muslin*

fabric marker

*needle and tacking
(basting) thread*

*30 cm x 90 cm
(12 in x 36 in) bronze satin*

*sewing machine and
matching thread*

cord or yarn

flat blunt needle

dressmaker's pins

*30 cm x 90 cm
(12 in x 36 in) blue satin*

dressmaker's scissors

press stud (snap fastener)

PREPARATION

Trace the design on to tissue paper. Tack (baste) the muslin to the wrong side of the bronze satin and stitch round the edge. Pin the template to the muslin and stitch the design. Cut and secure the ends and remove the template.

CORDED DESIGN 25%

1
Use the flat blunt needle to thread the cord or yarn through the channels. Pull the yarn out at the corners and leave a loop so as not to tighten and distort the fabric.

2
Right sides facing, pin to the blue satin. Stitch round the flap and across the opposite end. Clip and press to the right side. Slip-stitch the sides. Sew on the press stud (snap fastener).

CORDED QUILT

This method of quilting is worked by stitching the outline of a design in two parallel lines on to two layers of cloth. This creates channels which are then filled. This method can be worked all over for a whole cloth, or it can simply be used to make decorative borders.

YOU WILL NEED

dressmaker's scissors

satin fabric

muslin

tissue paper and pencil

dressmaker's pins

needle and tacking (basting) thread

sewing machine and matching thread

flat blunt needle

woollen yarn

calico for lining

PREPARATION

Decide on the size of your quilt and cut the satin and muslin to fit. Trace the design on to tissue paper several times until you have enough to make a complete border. Tack (baste) the muslin to the wrong side of the satin fabric and stitch round the quilt, close to the edge.

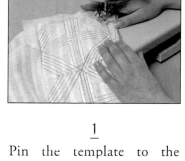

1

Pin the template to the muslin. Stitch the design in even parallel lines either side of the outline. Cut and secure the ends and remove the template.

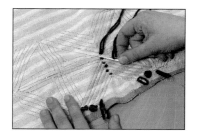

2

Thread the flat needle with yarn and insert it into a channel working the yarn between both layers of fabric. To turn a corner, bring out the needle to the wrong side, make a loop and then push back into the channel. Where two channels cross, cut the yarn and then continue on the other side. Fill the border of the quilt in this way.

TO FINISH

Trim the satin and muslin and cut the lining to fit. Right sides facing, stitch together, leaving a 10 cm (4 in) opening. Turn right sides out and slip-stitch the opening.

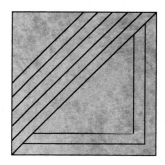

ONE-QUARTER OF DESIGN SHOWN. ENLARGE TO SIZE REQUIRED FOR QUILT.

SHADOW PICTURE

Shadow quilting is another form of trapunto work. This delightful child's picture is made from coloured shapes applied to a base. These are then covered with a transparent fabric, producing a delicate, shadowy effect.

25%

YOU WILL NEED
• • • • • •

paper and marker pen

dressmaker's scissors

double-sided tape

white, light and dark orange, and light and dark green felt squares

2 pieces muslin, each 38 cm x 30 cm (15 in x 12 in)

dressmaker's pins

needle and tacking (basting) thread

embroidery frame

white, orange, green and brown embroidery thread

crewel embroidery needle

iron

backing board

sticky tape

picture frame

PREPARATION

Enlarge the design on to paper, drawing the flower centres and the ladybird separately. Cut out all the pieces and stick them to the felt with double-sided tape. Draw round the shapes and cut out.

1

Lay a piece of muslin over the original drawing. Peel off the backing paper and position the felt pieces on the muslin. Place the second piece of muslin on top. Pin and tack (baste) the layers together.

2

Fit the work into an embroidery frame. Using a single strand of thread, stitch round all of the shapes in Holbein stitch (see Basic Techniques). Work details on to the snail, ladybird and flower centre in contrasting colours.

TO FINISH

Remove the quilting from the embroidery frame and press carefully on the reverse side. Use a backing board in a complementary colour to enhance the shadow quilting. Stretch the piece over the backing board, and tape it to the back. Place in a frame.

CAMEO PICTURE

This popular appliqué idea is fun to make. Copy a silhouette from a book or a piece of china and for unashamed plagiarism use a Wedgwood blue backing. A photograph of someone you know can also be used, so long as it is in profile. Mount the finished cameo in a frame or, alternatively, make a brooch following the instructions for the Gothic Jewels project.

YOU WILL NEED
• • • • • •

marker pen

fine white or black iron-on interfacing

dressmaker's scissors

iron

blue backing material

embroidery hoop

sewing machine and matching thread

small frame

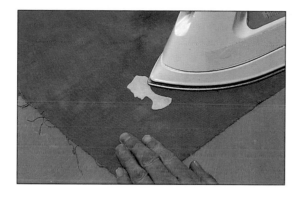

1
Trace the silhouette on to the interfacing. Cut out and iron on to the backing fabric.

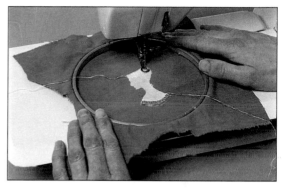

2
Stretch the backing material on an embroidery hoop. Remove the presser foot from your sewing machine and stitch round the outline. Add decorative details to the collar and hair to complete the design.

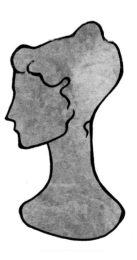

TO FINISH

Mount the finished cameo picture in a small frame (see Basic Techniques).

MIRROR FRAME

A patched fabric frame has been made from pieces of bronze silk, satin and organza. A quilted design and hand embroidery add a decorative touch.

YOU WILL NEED

dressmaker's paper and pencil

dressmaker's scissors

20 cm x 40 cm (8 in x 16 in) bronze satin

114 cm x 90 cm (45 in x 36 in) bronze silk

50 cm x 90 cm(20 in x 36 in) bronze organza

thick card (cardboard)

dressmaker's pins

sewing machine and matching thread

iron

needle and tacking (basting) thread

50 cm x 90 cm (20 in x 36 in) wadding (batting)

tissue paper

crewel needle and gold thread

30 cm (12 in) round mirror

multi-purpose glue

PREPARATION

Enlarge the templates from the back of the book and cut out in paper. Cut three strips from each of the bronze fabrics 40 cm (16 in) long. Vary the widths of the strips slightly, but plan so that when stitched together the combined width of all the strips is 50 cm (20 in). Cut out a backing board 3, in thick card (cardboard). Trace round the edge of 3, and from this cut a 10 cm (4 in) wide facing in bronze silk. Cut a piece 2 from the remaining silk.

1

Stitch together the satin, silk and organza strips, alternating the fabrics, and press the seams flat. From this, cut out piece 1 twice for the sides of the frame.

2

Cut out piece 2 in silk and place right sides facing the organza for the centre piece. Pin and stitch round the inner circle. Clip and trim. Turn right side out and press.

3

Right sides facing, pin the centre piece to the end sections and stitch. Clip the curves and trim the organza.

4

Tack (baste) the fabric to the wadding (batting) and trim to size. Enlarge and trace the quilted pattern from piece 3 on to tissue paper. Pin the paper to the fabric and machine stitch the design using matching thread. Add the stars freehand using gold thread. Pin and stitch the silk facing to the whole piece. Clip and press.

TO FINISH

Centre the mirror on the backing board 3 and glue. Cover the backing with the fabric frame. Fold the facing over to the wrong side of the backing and glue in place.

MEDIEVAL QUILT

This medieval-inspired quilt makes use of a harmonious colour scheme of frosty blues, soft golds and antique creams in glazed cotton, satin, brocade and moiré. The patches can be quilted individually, which is especially useful on a large-scale project such as this.

YOU WILL NEED

paper and pencil

dressmaker's scissors

fabric scraps in glazed cotton, brocade, satin and moiré

iron

dressmaker's pins

sewing machine and matching thread

calico

wadding (batting)

needle and tacking (basting) thread

thin card (cardboard)

craft knife

iron-on fusible bonding web

fabric scraps in metallic tissue and iridescent organza

crewel needle and thick metallic thread

beads and sequins

PREPARATION

This quilt is made up of 36 cm (14 in) square panels. Half of the panels have a large central diamond design and the other half are divided into four with either four diamond designs or two diamond and two square. Make a plan of the quilt and plan the colour fall. Enlarge the diagram and cut out a diamond template in both sizes, a triangular template in both sizes and a square template from paper. Cut out as many fabric patches as you need, adding a turning all round. Press under the turnings. Pin the patches together to form panels and machine together using zig zag stitch. Cut out the same number of panels in calico and wadding (batting). Sandwich the wadding between the patched fabric and the calico and tack (baste). Machine quilt the panels using zig zag stitch.

1
Enlarge and transfer the animal motifs from the back of the book to thin card (cardboard) and cut out. Iron the bonding web to the wrong side of the iridescent and metallic scraps. Cut out an animal motif for each panel with a large diamond design.

2
Peel off the backing paper and iron the motifs to the panels, then embellish with metallic thread, beads and sequins.

3
Hand quilt details on some of the panels using the thick metallic thread. On other panels, wrong side facing, machine quilt using thick metallic thread in the bobbin and regular thread on top.

PLAN AND TEMPLATES 25%

TO FINISH

To join the panels together, turn under the raw edges on the front and back and pin together. Zig zag the panels together from the back. Cut strips of calico about 5 cm (2 in) wide and as wide and as long as the quilt. Press under a turning along the long edges. Position the strips over the panel joins and top stitch to the front of the quilt using zig zag stitch. Make a border using calico and top stitch to the quilt in the same way.

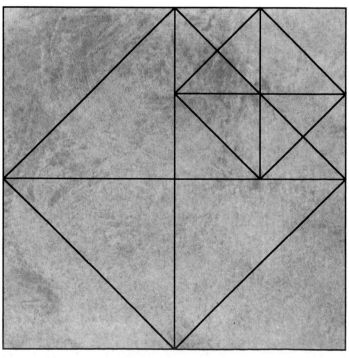

QUILTED WAISTCOAT

The paisley motif originated in India and was brought to Europe by the East India Company in the 18th century. A paisley design has been painted on to the waistcoat fronts and then each shape is hand quilted in stab stitch.

YOU WILL NEED
· · · · · ·

commercial waistcoat pattern

dressmaker's scissors

calico

black lining fabric

vanishing marker

gold gutta outliner

black, green and purple silk paint

paintbrush

wadding (batting)

needle and tacking (basting) thread

sewing machine and matching thread

PREPARATION

Cut out the waistcoat back and fronts in both calico and lining material. Enlarge the template from the back of the book and transfer the paisley design on to the calico fronts with the vanishing marker.

1
Outline the paisley design with the gold gutta outliner. Leave to dry overnight.

2
Fill in the pattern using the silk paints. Work one colour at a time and leave it to dry before starting the next colour. Then fill in the background colour.

3
Sandwich the wadding (batting) between the calico and the lining and tack (baste) in place. Work stab stitch round each motif to make it stand out (see Basic Techniques).

TO FINISH

Make up the waistcoat following the instructions with the commercial pattern.

QUILTED POCKET
· · · · · ·

A small project like this pocket is a good way to start quilting. Sew the finished pocket on to a plain shirt or a pyjama jacket.

YOU WILL NEED
· · · · · ·

*two 10 cm (4 in) squares
peach fabric*

*two 10 cm (4 in) squares
blue fabric*

*sewing machine and
matching thread*

iron-on interfacing

marker pen

dressmaker's pins

wadding (batting)

*needle and tacking
(basting) thread*

dressmaker's scissors

fabric scraps

sequins and beads

calico

PREPARATION

Enlarge the pocket template. Machine stitch the squares of fabric into a patched piece, alternating the colours.

POCKET AND MOTIF 25%

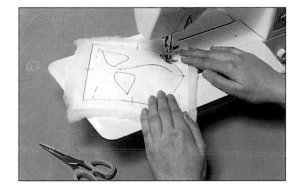

1

Enlarge and trace the motif on to the interfacing. Pin the interfacing to the wadding (batting), then machine stitch round the outline of the pocket. Tack (baste) the prepared wadding to the patch.

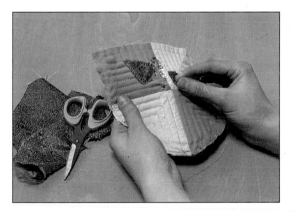

3

On the interfacing side, tack round the outline of the motif. Cut out the pieces for the motif in fabric scraps and hand appliqué to the pocket. Decorate with hand stitches and an assortment of sequins and beads.

TO FINISH

Cut the calico to fit the pocket and, right sides facing, stitch the calico back to the patched pocket leaving a small gap. Trim and clip the corners, turn right side out and press. Slip-stitch the opening. Position on the garment, and top stitch. Alternatively, if you are making the whole garment, the pocket back can be cut and applied as it is constructed.

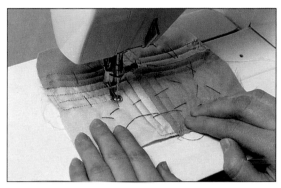

2

Machine stitch parallel lines round the inner sides of each fabric square. Machine stitch around the outline of the pocket and trim.

TRAPUNTO BOX

Trapunto, a very old art form, is by far the most admired form of quilting. Outlines are stitched to the fabric and then filled from the back. Quilt a Tudor rose in this way to cover a box lid.

YOU WILL NEED

dressmaker's scissors

*40 m x 90 cm
(16 in x 36 in) blue satin*

*30 cm x 90 cm
(12 in x 36 in) calico*

18 cm (7 in) hexagonal box

dressmaker's pins

*needle and tacking
(basting) thread*

vanishing marker

sticky back felt

*sewing machine and
gold thread*

wadding (batting)

fabric glue

50 cm (20 in) braid

PREPARATION

Cut the satin 40 cm (16 in) square. Cut a piece of calico the same size as the lid, and centre on the reverse side of the satin. Tack (baste) to secure in place. Enlarge and trace the template and draw the centred outline on to the satin with the vanishing marker. Draw round the base and sides of the box and round the base of the lid on to the sticky back felt. Cut out.

1
Machine stitch the outline of the Tudor rose in gold thread.

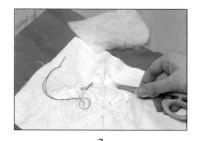

2
Slash the calico back of one petal and fill with wadding (batting). Stitch up the slit. Repeat on all shapes until the rose is full.

3
Centre the quilted design on the lid and glue. Stretch the satin over the lid and sides and stick the edges to the inside of the lid. Trim any excess. Cover the box in satin. Line the box with the sticky back felt. Glue the braid round the base of the box and round the lid.

50%

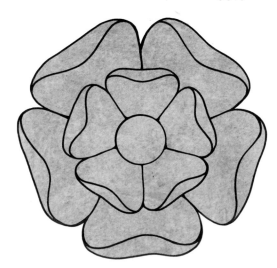

QUILTED BOX

The method used for the box lid illustrates simple machine quilting. Wadding (batting) is sandwiched between two layers and held together by the stitched outline of the diamond and fleur-de-lys motif.

YOU WILL NEED

vanishing marker

50 m x 90 cm (20 in x 36 in) gold satin

small rectangular box

wadding (batting)

dressmaker's scissors

needle and tacking (basting) thread

sticky back felt

sewing machine and matching thread

fabric glue

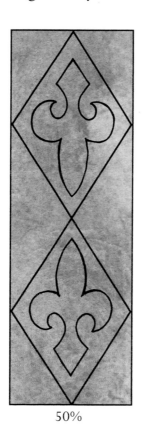

50%

PREPARATION

Enlarge the template and transfer the design with the vanishing marker on to a piece of gold satin, cut slightly larger than the lid. Cut the wadding (batting) to fit the lid. Centre and tack (baste) to the satin. Draw round the base of the box and lid on to the sticky back felt. Cut out.

<u>1</u>

Machine stitch the outline of the design.

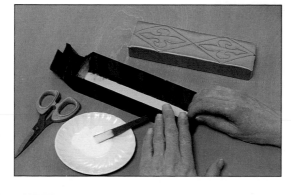

<u>2</u>

Glue the wadding (batting) to the lid. Fold the satin over the edge and inside the lid. Mitre the corners and glue. Cover the box in satin.

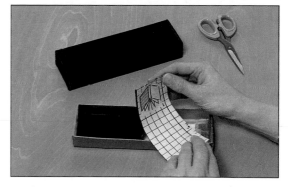

<u>3</u>

Attach the sticky back felt to the lid and the base of the box.

QUILTED HAT

This pull-on hat is made from wool and silk. The raised trapunto quilting on the hat band, in the form of diamonds, is embellished with bronze thread.

YOU WILL NEED
• • • • • •

*thin card (cardboard)
and pencil*

craft knife

dressmaker's paper

dressmaker's scissors

*50 cm x 90 cm
(20 in x 36 in) calico*

*50 cm x 90 cm
(20 in x 36 in) pink wool*

*50 cm x 90 cm
(20 in x 36 in) pink silk*

*sewing machine and
matching thread*

iron

dressmaker's pins

wadding (batting)

*crewel needle and bronze
thread*

*1 m x 90 cm
(1 yd x 36 in) silk lining*

*needle and tacking
(basting) thread*

*50 cm x 2.5 cm
(20 in x 1 in) petersham*

PREPARATION

Enlarge and cut out the motif templates in card (cardboard). Enlarge the hat templates from the back of the book and cut out piece 1 in calico and wool. Cut piece 2 in calico and silk. Cut crown piece 3 in wool and calico. Stitch pieces 1 and 2 together to make the hat band, first in calico, and then in wool and silk, taking a 1.5 cm (½ in) seam allowance. Clip and press the seams.

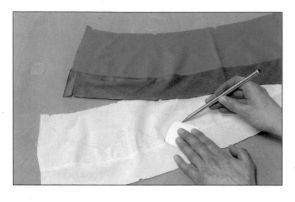

1
Draw round the templates on to the calico hat band, alternating the motif templates and spacing them evenly.

3
Wrong sides facing, pin together the two crown pieces. Pin and stitch to the quilted hat band. Turn right side out and top stitch close to the crown seam.

5
Tack (baste) the petersham band to the lower inside edge of the hat. Stitch and press under.

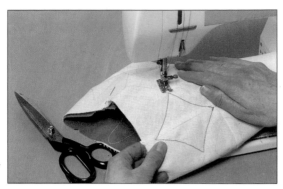

2
Stitch the ends of the hat band together and press. Wrong sides facing, pin the bands together and stitch round the motifs through both layers of fabric.

4
Turn inside out and carefully slash the calico behind each motif. Fill each motif with wadding (batting) then stitch closed. Embroider the diamonds with bronze stars. Make up a lining using the same pattern pieces and slip stitch in position.

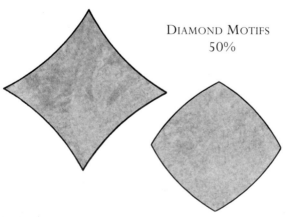

DIAMOND MOTIFS
50%

CRIB QUILT

Quilts like this were first made in the 19th century. Use washed out fabrics to achieve an old look. Pieces that look too bright can be sewn wrong side out. Beg or borrow scraps from friends and neighbours to make a family heirloom.

YOU WILL NEED

*thin card (cardboard)
and pencil*

craft knife

*assortment of cotton and
calico scraps*

dressmaker's scissors

*needle and tacking
(basting) thread*

iron

matching thread

*75 cm x 64 cm (30 in x
25 in) wadding (batting)*

*75 cm x 64 cm
(30 in x 25 in) calico*

dressmaker's pins

*crewel needle and ecru
embroidery thread*

*sewing thread in three
contrasting colours*

PREPARATION

Make two templates, one 8 cm (3 in) square and one 4 cm (1½ in) square. Cut 31 large and 128 small card (cardboard) squares. Cut the small patches from fabric scraps and the large patches from calico scraps, allowing for a 1 cm (½ in) turning on all sides. Tack (baste) the card squares to the patches. For the borders, cut two fabric strips 5 cm x 80 cm (2 in x 32 in) in three different colours, and two strips 5 cm x 65 cm (2 in x 26 in) in the same colours. Press a turning on the long sides of each strip.

1

Oversew the small squares into blocks of four. Alternate these blocks with the larger squares and oversew to make a quilt the equivalent of seven large squares wide and nine large squares deep. Remove tacking (basting) threads and the card (cardboard). Press the quilt seams open.

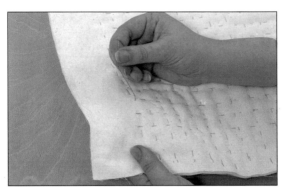

2

Place the patchwork face down and cover with wadding (batting) and calico. Pin the layers together, starting at the middle and gradually moving out. Tack the layers in lines of running stitches, removing the pins as you go.

3

To tuft the quilt, use embroidery thread to make a small stitch at the corners of each block and in the middle of the four square patches. Cut the threads to 4 cm (1½ in), securely knot and fluff out the ends with a needle.

4

Attach the borders to the front of the quilt with lines of running stitch in sewing thread using the Log Cabin method (see Basic Techniques). Mitre the corners (see Basic Techniques). Trim the raw edges, fold over and slip-stitch to the lining. Take the fabric over at the corners to show the Log Cabin effect.

STRING PATCHWORK FRAME

String patchwork is created by sewing similar lengths of fabric of different widths into one piece. Interesting effects are made by adjusting the angle of the strips and by making chevron shapes.

YOU WILL NEED

black and white satin

dressmaker's scissors

sewing machine and matching thread

two squares of thin card (cardboard)

craft knife

double-sided tape

masking tape

self-adhesive felt

needle

1

Cut the satin into narrow strips, varying the widths slightly. Right sides facing, machine stitch the strips together. Adjust the angles of the strips to make interesting effects.

2

Cut a window from one square of card (cardboard). Cut the patch into four sections to fit each side of the frame, allowing for a turning. Mitre the corners (see Basic Techniques).

TO FINISH

Stick the fabric to the frame with double-sided tape. Fold the raw ends to the inside and secure with masking tape. Cover the backing square with self-adhesive felt cut to size. Slip-stitch the front and back of the frame together round three sides.

STAINED GLASS APPLIQUÉ CUSHION

This cushion has been worked using the overlay method of appliqué. Keep design ideas bold and simple. It is also important that each shape within the design is not too small.

YOU WILL NEED

thin card (cardboard) and marker pen

48 cm (19 in) square red silk

dressmaker's pins

dressmaker's scissors

scraps of yellow and green silk

iron

iron-on interfacing

sewing machine and matching threads

tracing paper

transfer pencil

two 48 cm (19 in) squares black silk

craft knife

45 cm (18 in) square cushion pad

needle and matching thread

PREPARATION

Enlarge and transfer the template to the card (cardboard). Place the template over the red silk square and transfer the star outline, following the dotted lines, using pin prick marks. Cut along the pin pricks, without cutting the outer red frame. Make a template for each diamond shape and the centre piece, following the dotted lines. Draw round the templates on to the silk scraps. Cut four yellow and four green diamonds, and one red centre piece. Iron one piece of interfacing to the red frame.

1

Arrange the yellow and green diamonds and the red centre piece on the interfacing. Pin and iron in place. Machine stitch in place.

2

Following the continuous lines, trace the black frame on to tracing paper with a transfer pencil. Turn over and iron on to the second piece of interfacing. Iron the interfacing to the wrong side of one of the black silk squares. Cut out each diamond with a craft knife, leaving a small turning on all sides. Pin and press the turnings.

3

Pin the black frame on top of the appliqué star and machine along all the edges.

TO FINISH

Right sides facing, place the appliqué patch to the second black silk square and stitch a seam 1 cm (½ in) from the edges. Leave an opening. Clip the corners, press and turn right side out. Insert the cushion pad and slip-stitch the opening.

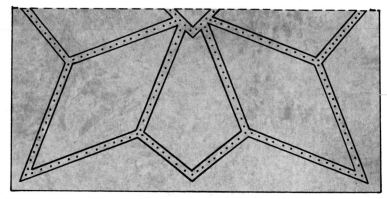

HALF OF PLAN SHOWN 25%

SILKEN BAG

This delicate piece of quilted silk sports a design of hearts, vine leaves and a bow surrounded by small running stitches. The finished quilt is sewn into a tiny drawstring bag.

YOU WILL NEED

dressmaker's scissors

40 cm x 90 cm (16 in x 36 in) lining silk

40 cm x 90 cm (16 in x 36 in) calico

tracing paper and pencil

8 cm x 30 cm (3 in x 12 in) wadding (batting)

needle and tacking (basting) thread

crewel needle and white perlé thread

sewing machine and matching thread

50 cm (20 in) cream silk ribbon

PREPARATION

Cut two pieces of lining silk and calico measuring 23 cm x 30 cm (9 in x 12 in). Enlarge and trace the design and transfer to one piece of silk. Sandwich the wadding (batting) between the two pieces of calico, positioning the wadding where you want the quilted design. Place the marked silk on top and tack (baste) the layers together.

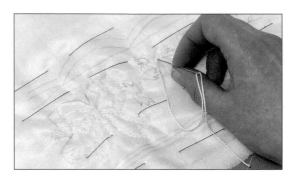

1

Outline the heart, vine and bow design in stab stitch (see Basic Techniques).

2

Work tiny running stitches round the design until the whole area has been covered.

REPEAT VINE AND HEART MOTIF ON OTHER SIDE OF BOW 50 %

TO FINISH

Cut 10 cm (4 in) diameter circle from lining silk and calico for the base of the bag. Make a lined drawstring bag using the remaining piece of lining silk and the base pieces (see Basic Techniques). For the channel, stitch two parallel lines 1 cm (½ in) apart with the top one 1 cm (½ in) from the edge. Thread and knot the silk ribbon.

BRODERIE PERSE APPLIQUÉ NAPKINS

This once popular craft was thought to closely resemble Persian embroidery. As it developed, more and more images were incorporated into the designs. A rose has been combined with a gardening fork to create these charming napkins.

YOU WILL NEED

tracing paper and pencil

scraps of plain grey, and pink and green floral chintz fabric

dressmaker's scissors

4 linen napkins

dressmaker's pins

needle and tacking (basting) thread

sewing machine and matching thread

iron

PREPARATION

Transfer the fork template from the back of the book to the grey fabric Add a small seam allowance and cut out. Cut out a flower shape, such as a rose, with a stem from chintz fabric, adding a small seam allowance.

1

Position the flower on a napkin with the stem entwined in the prongs of the fork. Pin and tack (baste) through the middle of the motifs. Turn under and tack a small turning and clip the edges as you work round the motifs.

2

Hand or machine stitch round the edges of the motifs to secure.

TO FINISH

Embellish all four napkins in the same way. Remove the tacking (basting) threads and press carefully. Embroider thorns on the rose stem in tiny stitches if desired.

BRODERIE PERSE
APPLIQUÉ TABLECLOTH

The technique of cutting out a design in printed cloth to appliqué to a fabric base grew out of both necessity and the desire to preserve old favourites. Appliqué chintz fabric with a large, floral motif to a linen cloth for an antique appearance.

YOU WILL NEED

dressmaker's scissors

Irish linen

dressmaker's pins

needle and tacking (basting) thread

sewing machine and matching thread

scraps of pink and green floral chintz fabric

iron

needle and matching thread

PREPARATION

Cut the linen to the shape and size you require. Turn under a small hem and stitch.

1
Draw a vase shape on to a scrap of chintz and cut out. Press under a small hem. Pin and tack (baste) to the corner of the cloth.

2
Cut a border in contrasting chintz. Press under a hem, pin and tack to the vase.

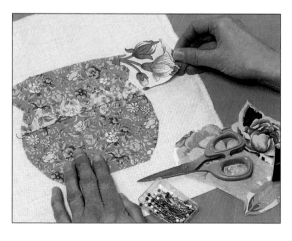

3
Cut out several flower shapes and leaves. Arrange in the vase, pin and tack in place.

4
Clip and turn the edges as you sew the motif to the cloth. When the shapes overlap each other, be sure to sew the base one first.

SILK DRESS

This technique uses up scraps of patterned silk. The silk patches are randomly joined into panels with French seams. The idea is to make enough patched squares to sew into a large piece of fabric, which is then made into a dress. Dye the dress a strong colour to unify the design.

YOU WILL NEED
· · · · · ·

dressmaker's paper and pencil

dressmaker's scissors

*scraps of fine silk or
silk scarves*

dressmaker's pins

*sewing machine and
matching thread*

iron

commercial dress pattern

cold water dye

PREPARATION

The panels measure 26 cm (10 in) square and they can be made up of patches following either or both diagrams. Enlarge the two diagrams and make templates for each shape and size of patch. Cut out patches from scraps of silk, allowing for a 1 cm (½ in) seam allowance on sides.

DRESS PANELS

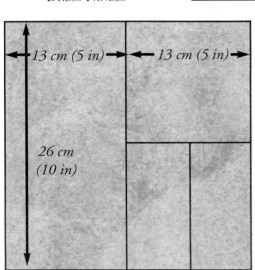

←13 cm (5 in)→ ←── 13 cm (5 in) ──→

26 cm
(10 in)

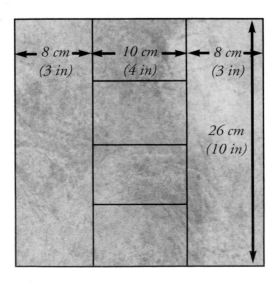

←8 cm
(3 in)→ ←─10 cm
(4 in)─→ ←8 cm
(3 in)→

26 cm
(10 in)

1

Using the flag method (see Basic Techniques), pin the patches in pairs with wrong sides facing. Machine and press the seams to one side. To make French seams, trim one edge back close to the stitching line. Press a small turning on the uncut edges, fold over again to cover the stitch line and press. Pin and stitch along the new fold.

2

Join the patches into panels, and the panels together in the same way to make a large piece of patched fabric.

TO FINISH

Cut out and make the dress following the instructions with the commercial dress pattern. Make up the cold dye solution, following the manufacturer's instructions. Then scrunch the dress up and dye.

CHILD'S SKIRT

Patches and strips of contrasting silk fabrics are sewn together in a creative mix to make this skirt. The appliqué silk patches sewn round the hemline add to the historic feel.

YOU WILL NEED
• • • • • •

thin perspex and marker

craft knife

dressmaker's scissors

1.2 m x 115 cm (47 in x 45 in) floral silk

scraps of contrasting silks

iron

dressmaker's pins

sewing machine and matching thread

needle and tacking (basting) thread

six buttons

PREPARATION

Enlarge and make the templates in perspex. Cut the floral fabric in half lengthwise. Cut two strips of contrasting silk 7 cm x 1.2 m (2½ in x 47 in), and press a 1 cm (½ in) seam allowance along the long edge. Cut four side strips in the same fabric, each 5 cm x 55 cm (2 in x 22 in).

TO FINISH

Halve the waist measurement and make two waistbands. Check the length of the skirt and trim if necessary. Gather the skirt on to the waistbands and top stitch. Make buttonholes and sew on the buttons.

1
Pin the templates to the silk scraps and cut out. Press under the seam allowances on patches.

2
Machine stitch one long strip to the wrong side of one piece of floral silk. Press over to the right side and top stitch. Repeat for the second piece. Attach the side strips in the same way.

3
Arrange the patches on the lower edge of the skirt, pin and tack (baste) in place. Machine stitch close to the edge.

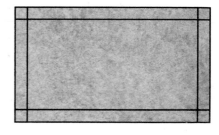

50%

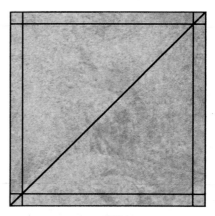

SATIN HANDBAG

This classic handbag is made from a piece of quilted satin. It has self-made handles and a quilted base for extra strength. Chose an unusual brass button to fasten the bag.

YOU WILL NEED

40 cm x 60 cm (16 in x 24 in) heavy interfacing

vanishing marker

dressmaker's scissors

40 cm x 60 cm (16 in x 24 in) wadding (batting)

40 cm x 60 cm (16 in x 24 in) satin

46 cm x 30 cm (18 in x 12 in) lining fabric

dressmaker's pins

sewing machine and matching thread

needle and tacking (basting) thread

iron

brass button

PREPARATION

Transfer the bag design from the back of the book to the interfacing. Cut out a piece of wadding (batting) to fit, and cut out the satin and a lining piece, adding a seam allowance on all sides. Sandwich the wadding between the marked interfacing and the satin, then pin and stitch round the edge. Machine quilt the grid. Cut out two satin and two lining side pieces and two satin handles, all with a seam allowance. Cut out an interfacing base 16 cm x 7 cm (6½ in x 2¾ in).

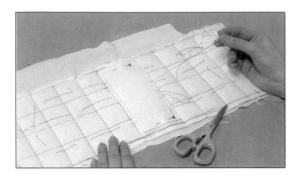

1

Position and tack (baste) the interfacing base to the bag. Trim the raw edges.

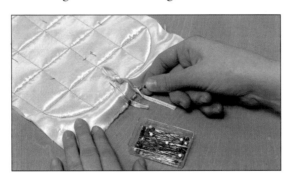

2

Make a narrow silk rouleau 5 cm x 20 cm (2 in x 8 in). Pin to the right side of the flap, with the loop pointing outwards. Make it big enough to fit the button. Right sides facing, pin the lining to the bag and stitch just inside the machine line, leaving an opening to turn through. Turn and slip-stitch closed.

3

Right sides facing, place satin and lining side pieces together in pairs. Machine round three sides, then turn through one long edge. Fold in half lengthwise and press. Machine stitch along fold to within 4 cm (1½ in) of the lower edge.

4

Top stitch round the base, the flap fold and the front edge of the bag.

5

Fold the handles in half lengthwise and press under a 1 cm (½ in) turning on both long sides and top stitch to 2.5 cm (1 in) of both ends. Open out the ends and top stitch to the bag.

TO FINISH

Slip-stitch the side pieces into the bag. Sew on a decorative button.

GOTHIC JEWELS

A plain velvet hat becomes a beautiful item of head wear when trimmed with sparkling Gothic jewels, made from machine embroidery and beads. The jewels do take time to make, however the extra effort is well worth the final result.

YOU WILL NEED
• • • • • •

marker pen
scraps of water soluble fabric
embroidery hoop
thick and fine metallic thread
sewing machine
scraps of tinsel fabric
wadding (batting)
dressmaker's pins
interfacing
dressmaker's scissors
needle and thread
pearl and glass beads

PREPARATION
Transfer the jewel designs on to scraps of water soluble fabric using the marker pen. Check your sewing machine manual for instructions on setting the machine for machine embroidery.

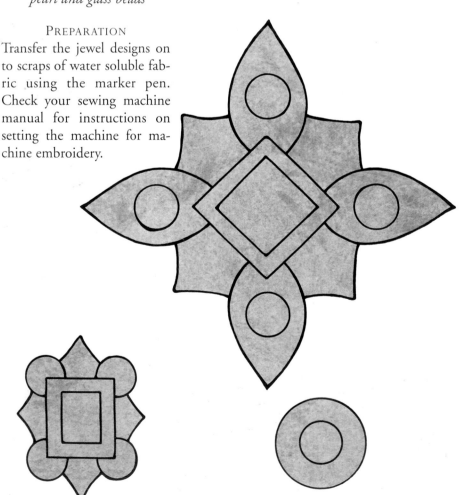

1
Stretch the water soluble fabric over the hoop. With the thick metallic thread in the bobbin, and fine metallic thread in the machine, stitch the outline. Fill in the shape with stitches, omitting the setting holes. Make one large and several small pieces.

2
Dissolve the water soluble fabric and leave the embroidery to dry. Place a scrap of tinsel fabric behind the embroidery. Push the wadding (batting) into the setting holes until the tinsel fabric projects through. Pin on a piece of interfacing, to hold it in place.

3
Machine round the wadding and cut away any excess fabric. Hand stitch pearl and glass beads round the edge of the setting. Decorate to your own taste.

4
Finally, slip-stitch the jewels to the top and brim of the hat.

COUNTRY STYLE

Create a nostalgic country mood with these soft textiles, full of associations with nature and folklore. Antique patchwork quilts were mostly made by country people and they often tell the story of the changing seasons, birds and flowers, weddings and births. They evoke an atmosphere of quiet comfort and hospitality. Choose cotton floral prints, ginghams, checks and stripes, mixing them together like an old-fashioned cottage garden.

INTRODUCTION

RIGHT: Beautiful quilts in soft colours epitomize country style. These are examples of French (left) and English (right) quilting designs.

BELOW: Two-colour quilts are both simple and striking. The Pineapple and Cherry Basket motifs are popular traditional patchwork designs.

Country style captures the spirit of a past, simple way of life, which revolved round the changing seasons. Quilts are very evocative, imbued with nostalgia for a slower pace of life, a sense of community and tranquillity. The detail of patchwork suggests time spent in simple pursuits, on long winter evenings. Patching and mending also give textiles nostalgic value and create a comfortable atmosphere. Unfortunately, as textiles decay, not many of us will have one of these treasures in the attic but you can derive deep satisfaction in making your own.

The rural idyll can be re-created by using the simple, adaptable motifs, styles and patterns which have inspired these step-by-step projects. Devised to suit all levels of competence and creativity, some require a minimum of stitching or no stitching at all. The motifs and patterns have been drawn from nature, tradition and religion. These potent images have symbolic meaning, with their roots in folklore. Certain animals, birds and plants traditionally have talismanic properties, which protect the house or person from bad spirits and endow them with good luck. Even apparently abstract patterns can be highly stylized images of recognizable symbols. The heart is the most well-known symbol of all, representing the universal emotion of love and friendship.

One of the best-loved designs in patchwork is the block pattern. A block is a square made up of patched pieces. The block can be repeated to make a pattern, and it can be assembled with a border or "sashing" between repetitions. This style crossed the Atlantic to the United States, where it became extremely popular. Motifs and patterns developed according to Amer-

ican traditions and folklore, but although the design known as Log Cabin was certainly named after an American method of house construction, it actually originated in England. Small strips are built up round a square, representing the timbers of a log cabin round the central hearth. Traditionally the block is divided diagonally into dark and light tones to echo the fire-light.

The very process of making a quilt became an excuse for social interaction. Settlers coming from their isolated homesteads would gather to eat, gossip and quilt. Often the patchwork would have been pieced beforehand, the patches then joined together into a whole piece or quilted as a group activity. This was inspired by a special family occasion like a wedding or birth, or to commemorate political events and victories. They often featured embroidered signatures and were often dated.

Bold geometric patchwork featuring large areas of solid colour is synonymous with the quiet Amish community, who have eschewed modern living. Their unusual colour combinations are quite unlike any other quilts.

Selection of appropriate fabrics is the key to a successful evocation of country style. Pure cotton fabric is an immensely practical fabric, being hardwearing and laundering well, easy to work with and available in many print designs. Cotton sateen, which has a subtle sheen, was traditionally favoured by quilters. To create a riot of colour and pattern, combine ginghams with stripes, checks or tiny florals which will appear as interesting tones in a large scheme. Choose plain colours with care, using historical examples and the shades of nature to inspire you. Turkey red was an extremely popular shade for patchwork. The colour is deep and bright, and teamed with white it is particularly striking. This combination is traditionally used for the Cherry Basket motif. Most importantly, do not be timid – colours need not co-ordinate as country style is often an eclectic collection of colours and patterns, and textiles will have faded and discoloured with the passage of time. To re-create that antique look, use an infusion of tea as a dye.

These step-by step-projects show you how to make individual heirlooms of your own. A handmade item is a very personal creation and will be highly prized; as a gift, it will always remind the recipient of the maker.

ABOVE: Even the most mundane of the 20th-century fabrics can evoke the country style. Here, old work shirts and pyjamas have been utilized.

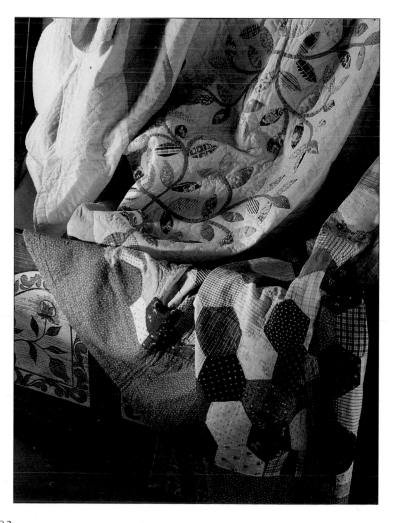

RIGHT: Two American quilts reveal gentle colour harmony. The one of the left is appliquéd (c. 1940) and the other is a 19th-century patchwork.

COUNTRY THROW

This delightful cotton throw is made from checked patches alternating with plain ones. This appliqué project lends itself to a country image with bold designs colouring plain squares.

YOU WILL NEED

60 cm x 90 cm (24 in x 36 in) calico

60 cm x 90 cm (24 in x 36 in) checked cotton fabric

dressmaker's scissors

tracing paper and pencil

20 cm x 90 cm (8 in x 36 in) iron-on fusible bonding web

iron

assortment of fabric scraps

dressmaker's pencil

crewel needle and assortment of embroidery threads

small glass beads

sewing machine and matching thread

1 m x 115 cm (40 in x 45 in) cotton drill

dressmaker's or safety pins

needle and tacking (basting) thread

shirt buttons

PREPARATION

Cut 13 calico and 12 checked cotton rectangles 17 cm x 19 cm (6½ in x 7½ in). Enlarge the motifs from the back of the book and trace on to the bonding web. Cut four hearts, three birds, two hands, and one pear, strawberry, grape and flower motif.

1

Roughly cut round the shapes on the bonding web and iron them on to the scraps. Cut out, peel off the backing paper and fuse to the calico squares.

2

Mark design details with a dressmaker's pencil and embroider round each shape. Use a variety of stitches and coloured threads. Sew on beads for the birds' eyes and holly berries.

3

Alternate checked with appliquéd squares in five rows, each row with five blocks. Use the flag method to join the blocks (see Basic Techniques), then join the rows.

4

Centre the patched piece on the cotton drill. Pin and tack (baste) through all the layers and round the outside edge. Stitch a small glass bead to each corner.

5

Press a 1 cm (½ in) hem round the outside edge, then fold in half to make a border. Pin, slip-stitch in place and mitre the corners (see Basic Techniques). Decorate the border with the shirt buttons.

AMISH BAG

· · · · · ·

The Amish people were already quilting when they first settled in America. Their simple designs are typically geometric with unusually dense stitching patterns. This envelope bag is patched and quilted in Amish style.

YOU WILL NEED

· · · · · ·

dressmaker's scissors

50 cm x 90 cm (20 in x 36 in) dark blue fabric

50 cm x 90 cm (20 in x 36 in) light blue fabric

50 cm x 90 cm (20 in x 36 in) dark green fabric

50 cm x 90 cm (20 in x 36 in) wadding (batting)

dressmaker's pins

sewing machine and matching thread

needle and tacking (basting) thread

red and green thread

2 m (2 yd) bias binding

press stud (snap fastener)

PREPARATION

Cut an 18 cm (7 in) square and four strips 24 cm x 6 cm (9½ in x 2½ in), from the dark blue fabric. Cut two 13 cm (5 in) squares in light blue fabric, then cut in half on the diagonal. Cut four 6 cm (2½ in) squares in light blue. Cut the border in the dark green fabric, with two strips 16 cm x 32 cm (6¼ in x 13 in), and two strips 16 cm x 60 cm (6¼ in x 24 in).

1

Pin and stitch the triangles to the large centre square with a 1 cm (½ in) seam allowance.

3

Attach the border to the patched piece (see Basic Techniques).

2

Pin and stitch the four strips and the small squares to the patched piece.

4

Cut the wadding (batting) and the backing fabric to fit. Layer the wadding, the patched piece and the backing, then pin and tack (baste) through all the layers. Machine a meandering filling stitch over the whole piece using the red and green thread.

TO FINISH

Bind the edges with bias binding (see Basic Techniques). Fold three corners into the centre like an envelope, pin and slip-stitch the binding. Sew a press stud (snap fastener) to both sides at the centre to close the flap.

PATCHWORK FRAME

Patchwork squares are sewn into strips to make the cover for this pretty picture frame.
Designed in checked fabric, it has its own naive style.

YOU WILL NEED

*two pieces of thick A4-size
card (cardboard)*

craft knife

fabric marker

scraps of wadding (batting)

dressmaker's scissors

double-sided tape

*20 cm x 90 cm
(8 in x 36 in) calico*

fabric glue

scraps of gingham

dressmaker's pins

*sewing machine and
matching thread*

iron

needle and matching thread

PREPARATION

Cut a window in one piece of
card (cardboard), with a 5 cm
(2 in) frame. The second piece
is for the backing board. Trace
the frame on to the wadding
(batting), cut out and stick together with double sided tape.
Draw round the backing
board on to the calico, and
cut out with a seam al-
lowance. Fold over the seam
allowance and glue to the
back. Cut a calico facing for
the inner and outer frame.
Cut the gingham scraps into
3.5 cm (1½ in) squares.

1

Pin the squares in pairs and
stitch with a 5 mm (¼ in)
seam allowance, using the flag
method (see Basic Tech-
niques). Make four strips of
10 patches, and four strips of
three. Sew pairs of strips together. Press and then join the
short strips to the long ones to
make a frame.

2

Right sides together, stitch the
facings round the inner and
outer frame. Clip the corners,
trim and press.

TO FINISH

Lay the fabric frame on the
card (cardboard), fold over the
facings and secure them with
double-sided tape. Put the
front and back of the frame
together and slip-stitch round
three sides.

APPLIQUÉ WOOL SCARF

A plain woollen scarf is appliquéd with unusual fabrics – suede, wool and corduroy.
Earthy colours compliment this organic motif.

YOU WILL NEED

tracing paper and pencil

thin card (cardboard)

craft knife

dressmaker's pencil

scraps of suede, corduroy and wool

dressmaker's scissors

rotary cutter

needle and tacking (basting) thread

30 cm x 150 cm (12 in x 60 in) wool fabric

sewing machine and matching thread

crewel needle and contrasting embroidery threads

PREPARATION

Enlarge and transfer the four motifs to the card (cardboard) and cut out.

1

Draw round the templates on to the fabric scraps with a dressmaker's pencil. Cut out the shapes using scissors, a rotary cutter or sharp craft knife. Tack (baste) the motifs to the scarf edge. Machine zig zag round the motifs.

2

Turn a hem on the long sides of the scarf and top stitch. Work large buttonhole stitch along the other two sides in a contrasting colour (see Basic Techniques). Embroider a few stitches on to the motifs.

MOTIFS 25%

SUNFLOWER SHELF EDGING

Shelf edgings decorating kitchen mantels were a common feature in country cottages in past times.
This shaped edging is appliquéd with cheerful sunflowers.

YOU WILL NEED
. . . . . .

*thin card (cardboard)
and pencil*

craft knife

*16 cm x 90 cm
(6½ in x 36 in) calico*

dressmaker's pencil

iron-on fusible bonding web

dressmaker's scissors

iron

*yellow, green and brown
gingham fabric scraps*

needle and cream thread

spray starch

pinking shears

PREPARATION
Enlarge and trace the template on to card (cardboard) and cut out with a craft knife.

1
Place the template at one end of the calico strip. Trace round the outline and repeat along the length of fabric.

2
Trace five flowers, five centres, and ten leaves on to the fusible bonding web. Iron on to the fabric scraps and cut round the outlines.

3
Peel off the backing paper and place two leaves above the first point on the calico. Place the sunflower on top, overlapping the leaves and iron in place. Work along the strip in this way using the points as guides.

4
Turn under the top edge and press a 1 cm (½ in) hem. Slip-stitch in place. Spray the piece with starch and then pink the marked line.

50%

BOLSTER CUSHION
• • • • • •

A patchwork bolster will make a stylish feature in any room as well as providing luxurious comfort.
The cover is fastened with buttons for easy removal on wash day.

YOU WILL NEED
• • • • • •

dressmaker's paper and pencil

dressmaker's scissors

iron-on fusible bonding web

iron

*50 cm x 90 cm
(20 in x 36 in) cotton fabric*

assorted fabric scraps

*sewing machine and
matching thread*

2 buttons

*45 cm x 18 cm (18 in x 7 in)
bolster pad*

PATCH TEMPLATE
50%

END PIECE 25%

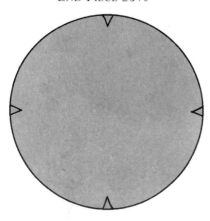

PREPARATION

Enlarge the end piece and copy on to paper. Cut a rectangle 47 cm x 70 cm (18½ in x 27½ in) and two end pieces in the main fabric. Draw eight patch templates on to the fusible bonding web. Iron to the fabric scraps and cut out. Press under a hem on both short sides of the main fabric piece and machine stitch. Make two buttonholes along one of these hemmed edges and iron the rectangular patches to one of the long edges. To make the patchwork base, cut the scraps into 7 cm x 4.5 cm (3 in x 2 in) rectangles and sew into short strips.

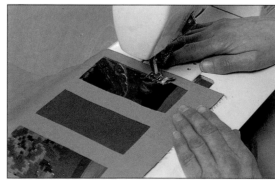

1

Set the machine to zig zag and outline each rectangular patch in satin stitch.

2

Pin and stitch the strips together to make a patch to fit the end piece. Lay the patch on one end piece, stitch round the edge and trim to fit.

TO FINISH

Pin the main piece into a tube. Insert the end pieces, sew, clip the curves and press. Turn right side out, and sew on the buttons. Insert pad.

COUNTRY WREATH CUSHION

"Ring a ring a roses . . ." This ticking cushion cover is decorated with posies arranged in a wreath.
The flowers are cut from an array of cotton fabrics and appliquéd to the cover in a ring.

YOU WILL NEED
• • • • • •

tracing paper and pencil

iron-on fusible bonding web

iron

assortment of fabric scraps

dressmaker's scissors

*45 cm x 95 cm (18 in x
38 in) striped ticking*

dinner plate

dressmaker's pencil

*assortment of embroidery
threads*

crewel needle

*sewing machine and
matching thread*

*45 cm (18 in) square
cushion pad*

PREPARATION

Enlarge the templates and
trace eight flowers, 18 flower
centres and 24 leaves on to the
fusible bonding web. Cut out
roughly and iron on to the
fabric scraps then cut round
the outline. Fold the ticking
into quarters to find the middle, centre a dinner plate on
top and draw round it with
the dressmaker's pencil.

1
Position the flowers on the
ticking in an even circle and
trace round them with the
dressmaker's pencil. Peel off
the backing paper.

2
Slip the leaves under the flowers – mix the colours, vary the
angles and iron in place. Fix a
centre on each flower and
arrange the extra circles round
the wreath to fill the gaps.

3
Using three strands of embroidery thread, work round
the edges of the shapes with
bold blanket stitches (see
Basic Techniques).

TO FINISH

Press under a 1 cm (½ in) hem
on both short ends and stitch.
Mark 25 cm (10 in) from one
edge, fold over the appliquéd
front and pin in place. Repeat
on the other side. Sew both
edges, clip the corners and
turn right side out. Insert the
cushion pad.

FLOWER AND FLOWER
CENTRE 50%

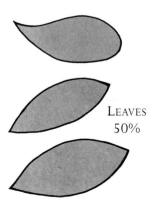

LEAVES
50%

CALICO RAG DOLL

Make a rag doll from some calico scraps and dress her up in patchwork clothes. The same template could be used to make another doll from a piece of patched fabric.

PREPARATION

Enlarge and trace the template from the back of the book and cut two shapes from the calico pieces, adding a 1 cm (½ in) seam allowance.

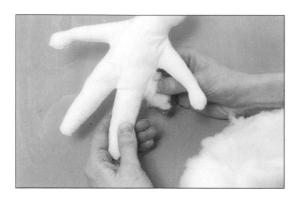

1

With right sides facing, pin and stitch the calico pieces together with a 1 cm (½ in) seam allowance. Leave a 4 cm (1½ in) gap under one arm. Clip the curves, trim any excess fabric and turn right side out. Fill the doll with polyester toy stuffing and slip-stitch the gap closed.

3

To make the body of the dress, cut 78 patches 3 cm (1¼ in) square from fabric scraps. Using the flag method, join in blocks of six (see Basic Techniques). Make a 13 row patchwork block. To make the sleeves, cut another 32 squares, and join four blocks in four rows, then make another the same. Press flat, and work running stitches either side of every seam. Join each block into a tube and hem the lower edge. Cut an angled opening either side of the dress and cut the sleeves to match. Sew in the sleeves.

2

Embroider the features and colour the cheeks pink. Make the hair by winding crochet cotton round the card (cardboard). Join with back stitch for the hair line, slip off the card and cut the other end. Sew to the head and twist into two plaits (braids). Secure with ribbons.

4

Put the dress on the doll. Gather the neck opening and trim with broderie anglaise. For the underskirt, make a broderie anglaise tube 11 cm x 22 cm (4½ in x 8½ in), run gathering thread to one end and sew to the doll's waist.

RAG BOOK

· · · · · ·

Over the years, rag books have retained their popularity as a safe and practical toy for small babies. This colourful book has ten leaves, filled with delightful appliqué motifs.

YOU WILL NEED
· · · · · ·

tracing paper and pencil

iron

iron-on fusible bonding web

assorted fabric scraps

dressmaker's scissors

60 cm x 90 cm
(24 in x 36 in) calico

20 cm x 90 cm (8 in x
36 in) floral cotton fabric

sewing machine and
matching thread

dressmaker's pins

PREPARATION

Select a range of simple and easy-to-identify images, together with letters and numbers. Trace on to the fusible bonding web. Iron to the reverse of the fabric scraps and cut out the shapes. Cut ten 20 cm (8 in) squares and a rectangle 14 cm x 17 cm (5½ in x 6½ in) in calico. Cut out two 20 cm (8 in) squares in floral fabric.

1

Remove the backing paper and iron the cut shapes to the calico squares.

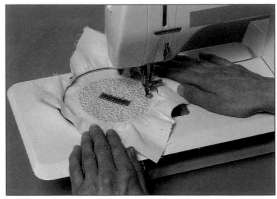

2

Set the machine to zig zag and secure with satin stitch. Make the picture for the front cover on the small calico rectangle, centre and stitch to one of the floral squares.

3

Pin and stitch the squares, right sides facing, to form pages. Back pages one and ten with the floral squares. Turn right side out and collate.

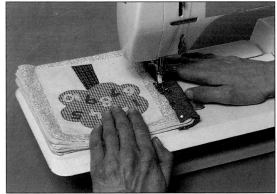

4

Cut a wide bias strip from the floral fabric to bind the spine. Pin and stitch the strip to the centre seam.

APPLIQUÉ T SHIRT
· · · · · ·

The flowerpot motif is easy to make. Brightly coloured fabric scraps in various prints are appliquéd to the front of a child's T shirt.

YOU WILL NEED
· · · · · ·

tracing paper and pencil

iron-on fusible bonding web

iron

assorted fabric scraps

dressmaker's scissors

needle and tacking (basting) thread

dressmaker's pins

plain T shirt

matching thread

<u>1</u>

Trace the templates on to the bonding web and iron to the fabric scraps. Cut out with a small seam allowance. Clip and tack (baste) under the seam allowance round all of the shapes.

<u>2</u>

Arrange the flowerpot motif on the T shirt, pin and slip-stitch in place.

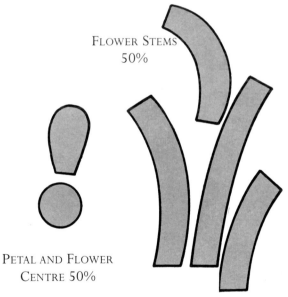

FLOWER STEMS
50%

PETAL AND FLOWER
CENTRE 50%

FLOWERPOT RIM 50%

FLOWERPOT 50%

AUTUMN LEAF SHOE BAG

Brightly coloured leaves, in autumnal shades, have been appliquéd in satin stitch to a calico drawstring bag. This bag is so charming that you could hang it on the back of a door in full view.

YOU WILL NEED

tracing paper and pencil

20 cm x 50 cm (8 in x 20 in) iron-on fusible bonding web

dressmaker's scissors

iron

assorted fabric scraps

50 cm x 56 cm (20 in x 22 in) cotton waffle fabric

sewing machine

red and cream thread

1 m (1 yd) narrow tape

safety pin

PREPARATION

Enlarge the templates and trace on to the fusible bonding web. Roughly cut out the shapes and then iron to the fabric scraps.

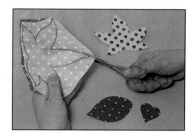

1

Carefully cut round the outline of each leaf and flower. Peel off the backing paper, arrange the shapes on the waffle fabric and iron on.

2

Set the machine to zig zag, and outline each shape in red satin stitch. Work a straight red line for the stems.

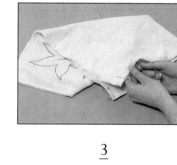

3

Right sides facing, make up the bag (see Basic Techniques), finishing the side seam 7 cm (2¾ in) from the top edge. Fold the top edge down 3 cm (1¼ in) and stitch.

LEAF TEMPLATES 50%

TO FINISH

Thread the tape through the channel using a safety pin. Tie the two ends together and trim the excess tape.

LITTLE HOUSE KEY RING

Keep your keys safe on this pretty key ring. The little house is made from tiny patched pieces which are appliquéd on to the fob.

YOU WILL NEED
· · · · · ·

tracing paper, paper and pencil

dressmaker's scissors

red and blue gingham and red fabric scraps

needle and tacking (basting) thread

iron

10 cm x 32 cm (4 in x 13 in) cream cotton fabric

10 cm x 15 cm (4 in x 6 in) wadding (batting)

red, cream and blue sewing thread

key ring

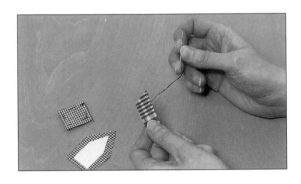

1

Trace the design on to paper and cut out two windows, two walls, two chimneys, a roof and a door. Cut out in scraps of fabric with a 5 mm (¼ in) seam allowance. Tack (baste) to the backing papers and press.

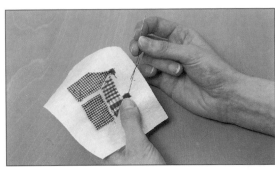

2

Cut two main pieces from cream cotton fabric and two from wadding (batting). Tack (baste) the house in sections to one piece of cotton fabric, removing the paper as you go. Slip-stitch with matching thread.

3

Sandwich the wadding between the appliquéd and plain fabrics, and tack through all the layers to secure.

4

Cut three bias strips in gingham (see Basic Techniques). Press under 5 mm (¼ in) turnings and bind the raw edges leaving 2.5 cm (1 in) free either side of the point. Thread the ends through the key ring and slip-stitch together.

KEY FOB AND
MOTIF TEMPLATE

HANGING HEART SACHET

Ever popular, lavender sachets are an ideal way to sweeten cupboards and drawers, leaving a freshness reminiscent of long, hot summer days.

50%

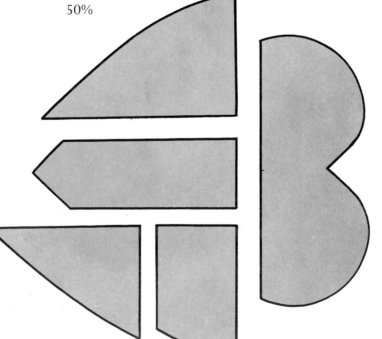

YOU WILL NEED
· · · · · ·

dressmaker's paper and pencil
scraps of cotton fabric
dressmaker's scissors
dressmaker's pins
needle and matching thread
iron
dried lavender
50 coloured glass beads
50 coloured headed pins
scrap of ribbon

PREPARATION

Enlarge the templates and make paper patterns. Cut out one of each shape from the fabric scraps.

1

Right sides facing, pin and stitch the pieces to make a heart shape, taking a small seam allowance. Trim the raw edges. Use the patched piece as a template to cut out another heart in plain fabric.

2

Right sides facing, pin and stitch round the heart, leaving a 5 cm (2 in) gap on one side. Clip the curves, press and turn right side out. Fill with lavender and slip-stitch the gap closed.

3

Thread the beads on to the coloured pins and space evenly round the edge. Sew a ribbon loop to the top.

HEART APPLIQUÉ PILLOWSLIP

Customize plain bed linen, to give it country appeal, by stitching appliqué hearts to a pillowslip.
Emphasize the hearts and raise the design with a halo of multi-coloured running stitches.

YOU WILL NEED

pencil and paper

25 cm (10 in) square iron-on
interfacing

dressmaker's scissors

iron

assorted scraps of brightly
coloured cotton

needle and tacking
(basting) thread

pillowslip

dressmaker's pins

matching thread

assortment of embroidery
threads

crewel needle

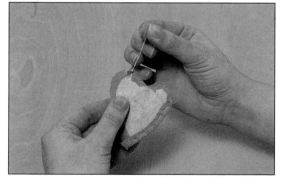

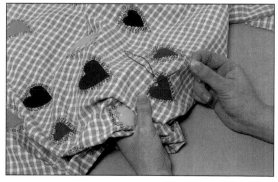

1

Draw 17 hearts, varying the sizes, on the interfacing and cut out. Iron the interfacing to the fabric scraps and cut out the shapes with a 5 mm (¼ in) seam allowance.

2

Clip the seam allowance round the curves, fold over and tack (baste) in place.

3

Arrange the hearts randomly on the pillowslip. Pin, tack and then slip-stitch in place. Using an assortment of coloured threads in one strand, work lines of tiny stitches around each heart in halos. Press to complete.

CHILD'S STRIP PATCHWORK RUCKSACK
· · · · · ·

Small children will love to carry their lunch to school in this practical rucksack. Floral and gingham fabrics are sewn into a patched piece, which is then quilted along the seams.

YOU WILL NEED
· · · · · ·

dressmaker's paper and pencil

dressmaker's scissors

60 cm x 1 m (24 in x 1 yd) wadding (batting)

1 m x 90 cm (1 yd x 36 in) gingham fabric

assorted floral and gingham cotton scraps

sewing machine and matching thread

needle and tacking (basting) thread

dressmaker's pins

1 m (1 yd) rope

wooden toggle

PREPARATION

Enlarge and trace the templates for a base and a flap on to paper. Make a paper template for the straps measuring 50 cm x 4 cm (20 in x 1½ in). Cut a rectangle 36 cm x 85 cm (14 in x 34 in) and a base, a flap and two straps in both the wadding (batting) and gingham. Cut a gingham casing for the rope tie 1 m x 10 cm (1 yd x 4 in), and a gingham bias strip 1.5 m x 4 cm (1½ yd x 1½ in). Cut the scraps into strips 6 cm x 36 cm (2½ in x 14 in). Taking a 5 mm (¼ in) seam allowance, sew the strips into a patched piece. From this cut a rectangle, a base, a flap and two straps. Lay the patchwork on top of the matching wadding and gingham pieces, tack (baste) through all layers and then quilt along the seam lines. Join the two short ends to make a tube. Centre the wadding along the gingham straps and fold the fabric round it. Turn under the raw edge, and stitch along the centre. Layer the patchwork, wadding and gingham base and flap pieces and quilt diagonally.

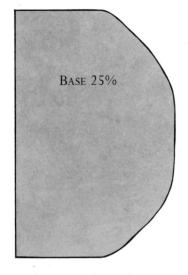

BASE 25%

FLAP 25%

TO FINISH

Thread the rope through the casing and knot. Make a narrow fabric rouleau and sew to the flap. Sew on the toggle.

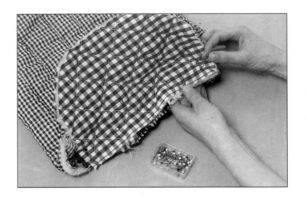

1

Wrong sides facing, pin the base to the tube. Insert the straps at either end, centred 5 cm (2 in) apart and pin to the bag. Bind the raw edges with the gingham bias strip.

2

Bind the top edge with the casing strip so that the ends meet at the centre front of the bag. Fold the binding over to right side, turn under a hem and top stitch below the previous seam.

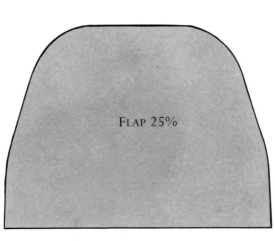

3

Bind the shaped edge of the flap with the gingham bias strip. Right sides facing, pin the flap to back of bag just below the casing. Stitch two rows, 1 cm (½ in) apart, close to the edge.

TOY BAG

Drawstring bags like this one make excellent storage space for all those tiny toys which most children seem to collect in large quantities. This bag has two rag dollies appliquéd on its pockets.

YOU WILL NEED
• • • • • •

tracing paper and pencil

iron-on fusible bonding web

iron

*red, green and cream
fabric scraps*

dressmaker's scissors

*70 cm x 115 cm (27½ in x
45 in) striped cotton fabric*

*20 cm x 90 cm (8 in x
36 in) checked cotton fabric*

*sewing machine and
matching thread*

small amount of brown yarn

lace scraps

*blue and red embroidery
thread*

crewel needle

dressmaker's pins

3 m (3 yd) cord

PREPARATION

Trace as many shapes as you need to make two dolls on to the fusible bonding web. Iron on to the fabric scraps and cut out. Cut out a rectangle 70 cm x 100 cm (27½ in x 40 in) in the striped fabric, and two pockets 20 cm x 25 cm (8 in x 10 in) in the checked fabric.

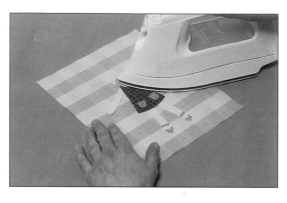

1
Assemble the fabric shapes and iron on to the pockets to make two dolls. Secure the pieces with machine zig zag. Sew lengths of yarn for hair and a scrap of lace on the dress hem. Sew blue french knots for eyes and sew a red smile.

3
Pin and stitch the bag along two sides. Fold over 10 cm (4 in) along the top edge and press.

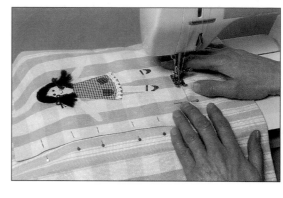

2
Hem the long side of the striped fabric, fold in half and press. Hem the pocket tops, and press under the seam allowance on the other three sides. Pin the pockets to the front of the bag and top stitch in place.

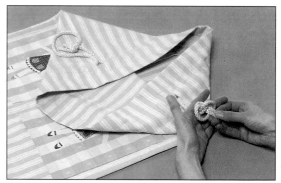

4
Make two buttonholes each side of the seam, 15 cm (6 in) from the top edge. Stitch a line either side of the buttonholes. Cut the cord in half, thread through the buttonholes and knot.

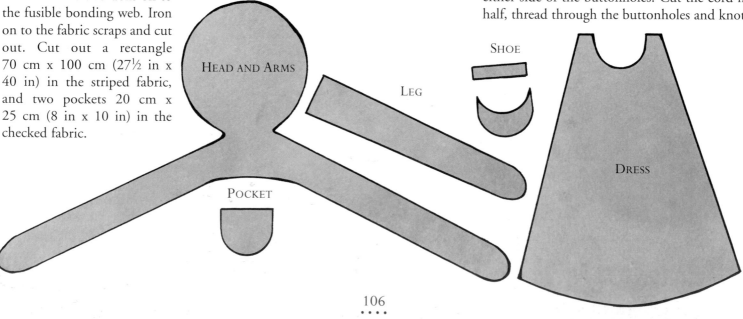

HEAD AND ARMS

LEG

SHOE

POCKET

DRESS

CHILD'S STRIP PATCHWORK WAISTCOAT
· · · · · ·

This waistcoat is made from patched strips. You can use long, narrow and seemingly useless pieces of fabric left over from previous projects. Fold the fabric like a concertina and cut into strips. Try to use strips that are somehow linked, either by colour tone or the size of the print.

commercial waistcoat pattern

assorted floral scraps

dressmaker's scissors

*sewing machine and
matching thread*

iron

*85 cm x 90 cm
(34 in x 36 in) plain fabric*

dressmaker's pins

needle

4 buttons

PREPARATION

Fabric amounts are given for a waistcoat to fit chest 64 cm (26 in). To make the patched piece, join five 6 cm x 90 cm (2½ in x 36 in) strips, taking a 5 mm (¼ in) seam allowance. Halve the patched piece and cut out two waistcoat fronts. Cut two backs, two fronts and two interfacings in plain cotton.

1

Right sides facing, machine the interfacings to the fronts and press the seams. Stitch the fronts to the back. Make up the lining and pin to the waistcoat, matching shoulder seams. Stitch round the outer edges leaving the side seams open. Trim the edges and clip.

2

Turn the waistcoat right side out and press. Pin the back to the fronts at the side seams and stitch, leaving a small gap. Clip and press open the seam allowances.

3

Make four evenly spaced buttonholes on the right front and sew four buttons to the left.

CHILD'S STRIP PATCHWORK SKIRT

This gathered skirt is made from pieced strips to match the child's waistcoat. The skirt is finished with a double hem band made from a floral and striped patchwork strip.

YOU WILL NEED

dressmaker's scissors

assorted scraps of floral and striped fabric

sewing machine and matching thread

40 cm x 160 cm (16 in x 63 in) plain fabric for lining

iron

needle

dressmaker's pins

elastic

PREPARATION

Fabric amounts are given for a skirt to fit waist 58 cm (23 in), with a back length of 50 cm (20 in). To make the patched piece, cut 32 strips 6 cm x 40 cm (2½ in x 16 in) from the floral and striped fabrics. Join together, taking a 5 mm (¼ in) seam allowance. Cut a striped and floral strip 6 cm x 160 cm (2½ in x 63 in) and join, long sides together, for the hem band. Right sides facing, join one edge of the hem band to the base of the skirt and the other to the lining fabric. Press and turn right sides out. For a waistband, cut a piece 12 cm x 80 cm (4¾ in x 31½ in).

1
Sew two rows of running stitch 5 mm (¼ in) and 1.5 cm (½ in) from the top of the skirt. Pull up the threads to gather the skirt to the size of the waistband.

2
Pin the waistband to the gathered edge and stitch. Fold over to the right side and pin. Top stitch along the waistband, just below the previous seam line, leaving a gap. Thread the elastic through the waistband and secure.

LOG CABIN THROW

The Log Cabin is a traditional patchwork design. While you can use any number of colours, choosing a limited combination is probably the best way to unify the whole design.

YOU WILL NEED

dressmaker's scissors

20 cm x 90 cm (8 in x 36 in) blue needlecord (fine-wale corduroy)

1 m x 90 cm (1 yd x 36 in) red needlecord (fine-wale corduroy)

assortment of floral fabric scraps in red and blue

2 m x 2.5 m (2½ yd x 3 yd) plain blue fabric

dressmaker's pins

sewing machine and matching thread

iron

2 m x 2.5 m (2½ yd x 3 yd) red floral backing fabric

PREPARATION

The finished piece measures 1.8 m x 2.3 m (71 in x 90½ in) and is made from 12 blue pieced centres, six red pieced centres and 17 plain blue squares. It is edged with three borders. Cut out 12 blue and six red needlecord (fine-wale corduroy) 10 cm (4 in) squares. Cut the floral scraps, and some blue and red needlecord into strips 4 cm (1½ in) wide. Cut 17 plain blue 32 cm (13 in) squares. For the borders cut four red floral strips and four blue needlecord (fine-wale corduroy) strips 8 cm (3 in) wide. The pieced centres are worked from the middle out.

1

Sew a blue needlecord square to a red floral strip and trim even with the square. Sew a red floral string across the top edge of the pieced centre and trim even with the pieced centre. Sew a red floral strip to the left edge and trim.

2

To complete the centre, sew a fourth red floral strip to the lower edge, trim and press.

TO FINISH

Sew the borders to the patched piece (see Basic Techniques). Lay on top of the backing piece and, starting in the middle, tack (baste) through all the layers. Stitch round each pieced square to outline the quilt. Trim the backing to overlap the patchwork all round by 13 cm (5 in). Fold the backing over to the front of the throw to make an outer border. Turn under the raw edges and top stitch. Mitre the corners if wished (see Basic Techniques).

3

Continue to add strips round the centre. First add the blue floral strips, then the red floral strips and finally with the blue needlecord strips. Press and trim to 32 cm (13 in) square. Make up twelve blue centred squares and six red centred squares, alternating red and blue floral strips.

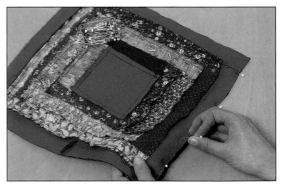

4

Sew a blue pieced centre to a plain blue square using the flag technique (see Basic Techniques). Repeat, until four blue pieced centres are separated by three plain blue squares. Make two more rows the same, then two rows with three red pieced centres separated by four plain blue squares. Join the rows so the colours alternate.

PATCHWORK TEA AND EGG COSIES

This matching tea and egg cosy set is made from strips of tartan fabric which have been quilted down the seam lines.

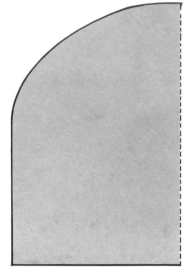

YOU WILL NEED
• • • • • •

dressmaker's paper and pencil

dressmaker's scissors

51 cm x 90 cm (20 in x 36 in) wadding (batting)

assorted scraps of tartan cotton fabric

sewing machine and matching thread

30 cm x 90 cm (12 in x 36 in) cotton lining fabric

dressmaker's pins

12 cm (4½ in) of 1 cm (½ in) tartan ribbon

PREPARATION

Fabric amounts are for one tea cosy and two egg cosies. Enlarge the templates and cut out two large and four small pieces in wadding (batting). Cut the scraps into 12 cm (5 in) strips and stitch with a 5 mm (¼ in) seam allowance into one piece. Cut four small and two large pieces in patchwork and lining fabric. Pin one patched piece to the wadding and machine quilt along the seam lines. Trim the edges and repeat with the other side. Sew a ribbon loop to the centre top of one side.

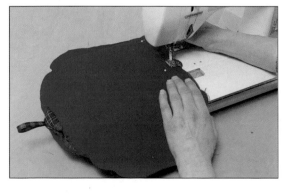

1
Right sides facing, pin the two sides together and stitch round the top and sides.

2
Stitch the linings together leaving a gap at the top. Place the cosy inside the lining, right sides together. Pin and stitch along the lower edge, turn right side out and slip-stitch the opening.

3
Push the lining inside the cosy leaving a band on the right side. Top stitch along the seam line.

NAPKIN AND NAPKIN RING

Get set for lunch with these co-ordinating accessories, appliquéd with fabric scraps and decorated with big wooden buttons. Ambitious enthusiasts might even attempt a matching table cloth.

YOU WILL NEED

iron

iron-on fusible bonding web

assorted blue and blue and white fabric scraps

dressmaker's scissors

sewing machine and matching thread

linen or cotton napkin

strips of calico scraps

navy embroidery thread

crewel needle

needle and matching thread

5 wooden buttons

PREPARATION

For the napkin, iron the bonding web to the assorted scraps and cut into 6 cm (2½ in) squares. Cut four plain blue 6 cm (2½ in) squares and, right sides facing, stitch to each corner of the napkin along two sides. Cut four calico strips as long as the napkin and 6 cm (2½ in) wide. Iron the assorted squares to the calico strips.

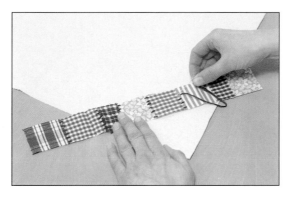

1

Work large navy stab stitches along the seam lines between each square (see Basic Techniques). Right sides facing, machine the four strips along the edges of the napkin. Turn right side out and press.

2

Work navy stab stitch along all four edges and sew a button in each corner. Make the napkin ring in the same way from two patched strips. Make a buttonhole on one short edge and sew a button to the other.

DRESDEN PLATE HERB CUSHION

This small scatter cushion is made from a ring of patched pieces which copy the design of a Dresden plate. Fill the cushion with dried herbs or lavender to entice you gently to sleep.

YOU WILL NEED

1 m x 90 cm
(1 yd x 36 in) calico

dressmaker's scissors

pencil and paper

card (cardboard)

craft knife

assorted scraps of patterned fabric, in blue, mauve and white

embroidery scissors

needle and tacking (basting) thread

31 cm (12¼ in) square wadding (batting)

pale and dark purple embroidery thread

crewel needle

2 m (2 yd) of 5 mm (¼ in) lilac ribbon

sewing machine and matching thread

1 m x 90 cm
(1 yd x 36 in) muslin

dried herbs or lavender

PREPARATION

Cut one 33 cm (13 in) square in calico.

1

Trace the design from the back of the book on to the paper, then make templates of all the shapes in card (cardboard). Cut out of fabric scraps, adding a 5 mm (1/4 in) seam allowance. Tack (baste) the fabric scraps to the card templates, fold over the edges and whip stitch together (see Basic Techniques). Remove the tacking threads and templates.

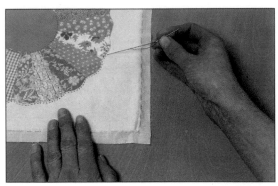

2

Centre the finished patchwork on the calico square, right side uppermost, with the wadding (batting) sandwiched between. Tack through all three layers. Outline all the shapes in running stitch, using both shades of embroidery thread.

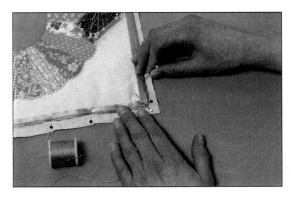

3

Pin the ribbon round the cushion square and top stitch along both edges, mitring the corners (see Basic Techniques).

TO FINISH

Cut two pieces of calico 33 cm x 18 cm (13 in x 7 in) for the backing and make a envelope cushion cover (see Basic Techniques). Cut two square pieces of muslin slightly smaller than the cushion and stitch together, leaving one side open. Fill with herbs or lavender and slip-stitch the opening. Insert the pad inside the cushion cover.

4

Cut a calico strip 13 cm x 3 m (5 in x 3 yd), joining the fabric as necessary, and hem one long edge. Stitch two rows along the other edge and pull up the threads to gather into a frill. Right sides facing, pin the frill to the cushion and stitch.

PATCHWORK CARDS

Patchwork designs like this Northumberland star can be used to make unusual gift cards.

YOU WILL NEED
......

tracing paper and pencil
ruler
iron-on fusible bonding web
iron
assortment of fabric scraps
dressmaker's scissors
coloured card (cardboard)
metallic marker pen

PREPARATION

Work out a design on paper. Trace the design on to the bonding web.

1

Cut out the shapes. Iron the shapes on to the back of the fabric scraps and cut out without a seam allowance.

2

Lay the shapes on the card (cardboard) to make up the design. Cover with a clean cloth and iron. Outline the design with the marker pen.

PHOTO FRAME

Blue and white checked fabrics make a fresh looking border for a favourite photo. Appliqué a pretty flower to each corner.

YOU WILL NEED

two pieces of thick card (cardboard), 22 cm (8 in) square

craft knife

scraps of blue and white gingham and checked fabric

dressmaker's scissors

scraps of cream fabric

iron

iron-on fusible bonding web

assorted scraps of fabric for the flowers

green and navy embroidery thread

crewel needle

dressmaker's pins

needle and matching thread

fabric glue

double-sided tape

PREPARATION

Cut out a centre square from one piece of the card (cardboard), leaving a 5 cm (2 in) border. Cut four gingham border strips 27 cm x 10 cm (11 in x 4 in). Cut four 7 cm (3 in) squares of cream fabric and press under the raw edges to make 5 cm (2 in) squares. Iron bonding web to the reverse of the fabric scraps and cut out four flower shapes and four pairs of leaves.

1

Pull off the backing from the bonding web and iron a flower and leaves motif to the corner of each cream square, as shown. Embroider the stems in green thread. Cut four narrow strips of checked fabric 27 cm (11 in) long and press under the long edges. Pin and stitch along the centre of the gingham borders.

2

Glue the cream squares to the corners of the frame where the borders meet, with the flowers facing outwards. Work large stab stitches round the squares in navy thread (see Basic Techniques). Fold the border fabric over to the back of the frame and secure with double-sided tape. Cover the other piece of card with fabric then slip-stitch the two pieces together round three sides, leaving one side open to insert the photo.

DIAMOND IN A SQUARE QUILT
· · · · · ·

Using the Log Cabin technique, offset a centre square with four triangles to make a traditional
Diamond-in-a-Square. The finished piece is edged with a magnificent sawtooth border.

YOU WILL NEED
· · · · · ·

*assorted red and blue printed
cotton fabric*

dressmaker's scissors

*3 m x 90 cm (3 yd x 36 in)
red cotton fabric*

*4.5 m x 115 cm (5 yd x
45 in) blue cotton fabric*

dressmaker's pins

*sewing machine and
matching thread*

iron

*9 m (9 yd) of 2 cm (¾ in)
blue ribbon*

*needle and tacking
(basting) thread*

PREPARATION

The finished wall hanging measures 2 m x 2.5 m (6½ ft x 8 ft) and is made from 12 blue patchwork
centres, six red patchwork centres, and 17 plain squares. From the printed fabric, cut out 93 red
and 94 blue 15 cm (6 in) squares. Cut red and blue printed strips 8 cm (3 in) wide, you need four
for each block (see Method 1). Make a plain blue border 8 m x 8 cm (8¾ yd x 3 in). For the
sawtooth border, make a plain red strip 9 m x 20 cm (10 yd x 8 in) and press in half lengthways.
Press under a 5 mm (¼ in) hem on the top edge and mark at 7 cm (2¾ in) intervals, 4.5 cm (1¾ in)
below the fold line and 3 cm (1¼ in) from the top. Stitch from point to point. Cut triangles out of
the folded edge, close to the stitching, and clip into the corners. Turn right side out and press.

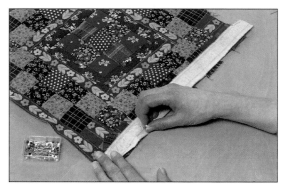

1

Using the flag method (see Basic Techniques)
join three squares to make a row and then three
rows to make a nine-patch block. Sew a blue
strip to both short and long sides, and trim.
Sew four red strips to the block in the same
way. Join five squares to make a row, make
another the same and stitch either side of the
patchwork centre. Make two rows of seven
squares to complete the square. Pin and stitch
a border of the red strip to the square. Make
two more identical squares.

2

For the sawtooth border, press two of the
pieced patchwork squares diagonally in half.
Cut along the fold to make four triangles, pin
and stitch to the square. Make two rows of 14
squares and join to both ends.

3

Pin the ribbon along the raw edge of the
sawtooth border. Top stitch along both edges
of the ribbon.

TO FINISH

Right side facing, stitch the blue border round
the patchwork (see Basic Techniques). Cut a
backing from the plain blue fabric to fit and lay
the patchwork on top. Starting in the middle,
tack (baste) through all layers. Outline the quilt
with lines of machine stitch. Stitch the
sawtooth border to the backing, fold to the
front and top stitch.

CHERRY BASKET PATCHWORK CUSHION

The cherry basket used to decorate this striking cushion is a traditional patchwork design. Make it in plain contrasting colours, or in pretty prints for a completely different look.

YOU WILL NEED
• • • • • •

paper and pencil

card (cardboard)

craft knife

scraps of red and white cotton fabric

dressmaker's scissors

38 cm x 90 cm (15 in x 36 in) cotton poplin

38 cm (15 in) square wadding (batting)

needle and tacking (basting) thread

dressmaker's pins

needle and matching thread

25 cm (10 in) square iron-on interfacing

iron

backing fabric

sewing machine and matching thread

square cushion pad

PREPARATION

Enlarge the triangle from the back of the book and cut out 18 card (cardboard) templates. Cut out 12 triangles in red fabric and six in white fabric, adding a 5 mm (¼ in) seam allowance. Cut out two 38 cm (15 in) squares in cotton poplin. Tack (baste) the wadding (batting) to the reverse of one square.

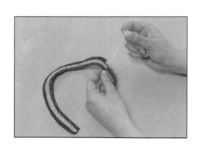

1

Pin and sew the triangles in pairs. Join eight triangles into a square, then join four more to the two top corners to make a large triangular shape. Follow the photographs for reference.

2

Pin the basket to the prepared poplin square, fold under the seam allowance and slip-stitch in place. Slip-stitch the two remaining triangles to make the base.

3

Draw a semi-circle on the interfacing with a 25 cm (10 in) base line and use this to cut out a handle 1 cm (½ in) wide. Iron on to a scrap of red fabric. Cut out, adding a 5 mm (¼ in) seam allowance, fold under the seam allowance and slip-stitch to the top of the basket.

TO FINISH

Work stab stitch round each triangle and the basket handle. Make a cushion cover (see Basic Techniques). Insert the cushion pad.

HEXAGON PIN CUSHION

Make this boldly patterned pin cushion from navy and white fabrics.

YOU WILL NEED

*assorted plain and print
scraps of navy fabric*

tracing paper and pencil

card (cardboard)

craft knife

dressmaker's pins

*needle and tacking
(basting) thread*

matching thread

wadding (batting)

PREPARATION

Enlarge and trace the hexagon on to paper and cut out 14 card (cardboard) templates. Cut out two plain navy patches, and four patches in three other navy fabrics, adding a 5 mm (¼ in) seam allowance. Pin and tack (baste) the patches to the card templates.

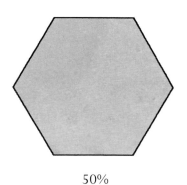

50%

1

Join the hexagons into two flower shapes, with six patterned patches round a central navy patch. Oversew the piece neatly. Make a second flower shape the same way.

2

Wrong sides facing, pin and tack (baste) the two pieces together. Slip-stitch round the outside edge, leaving a small gap. Turn right side out. Fill with wadding (batting) and then slip-stitch the gap.

121

CRAZY PATCHWORK BOOTEES
• • • • • •

These pull-on quilted booties have tops made from tiny pieces of crazy patchwork. Lined with ging-ham and secured at the top with elastic, they are a warm and comfortable gift for a baby.

YOU WILL NEED
• • • • • •

paper and pencil

paper scissors

20 cm x 90 cm (8 in x 36 in) blue cotton denim

20 cm x 90 cm (8 in x 36 in) gingham fabric

dressmaker's scissors

scrap of wadding (batting)

assorted blue fabric scraps

dressmaker's pins

needle and tacking (basting) thread

sewing machine and matching thread

elastic

50 cm (20 in) bias binding

PREPARATION

Enlarge the pattern pieces from this page and from the back of the book. Cut out two tops, two soles and two front and side pieces in denim. Cut out two soles and four linings in gingham, and two soles in wadding (batting).

1
Cut small scraps of blue fabric and tack (baste) to the bootee tops, turning under the edges. Secure with machine zig zag stitch.

2
Stitch the lining pieces together along the two short edges.

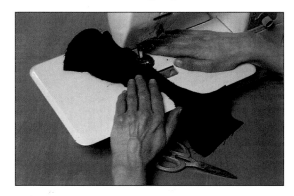

3
Right sides facing, insert the patchwork top into the denim front and side pieces. Pin the elastic along the top edge and stitch. Join the back seam. Right sides facing, attach the lining to the top edge, clip and turn through.

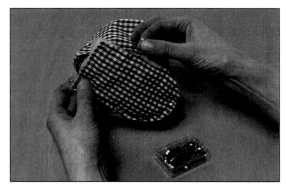

4
Sandwich the wadding (batting) soles between the denim and gingham soles. Tack through all the layers. Turn the bootees inside out, and pin and stitch the soles in place. Cover the seams with bias binding to neaten.

FRONT AND SIDES 50%

LINING 50%

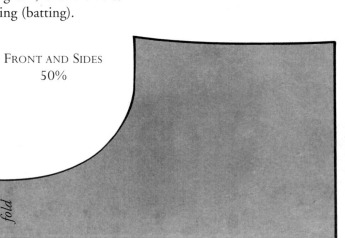

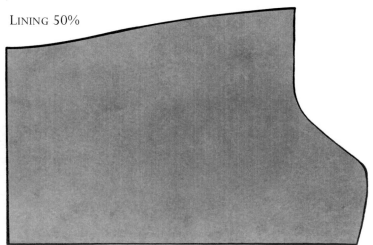

fold

SMALL QUILT

This richly coloured quilt will fit a doll's bed, but it is also large enough for a Moses basket or a baby's crib. This project uses a clever method to secure the appliqué parts until they are needed.

YOU WILL NEED
•••••••

50 cm x 90 cm (20 in x 36 in) contrasting fabric

dressmaker's scissors

sewing machine and matching thread

50 cm x 65 cm (20 in x 26 in) main fabric

paper and pencil

card (cardboard)

paper scissors

assorted fabric scraps

iron-on interfacing

tissue paper

iron

needle and tacking (basting) thread

10 cm x 90 cm (4 in x 36 in) assorted green cotton fabric

matching thread

50 cm x 65 cm (20 in x 26 in) wadding (batting)

50 cm x 65 cm (20 in x 26 in) backing fabric

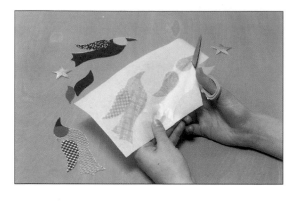

1
Lay the fabric pieces for each bird on to the interfacing, cover with tissue paper and iron – this keeps the pieces together. Prepare all the birds in this way and cut them out.

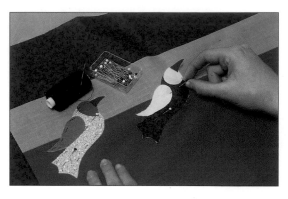

2
Arrange the birds on the quilt in rows. Tack (baste) the pieces on top of each other and secure with a small machine zig zag stitch.

3
Cut a 2 cm (¾ in) wide bias strip in green cotton. Press in half lengthways, and stitch along the fold. Fold over to cover the stitches and press. Trim back to the seam line.

4
Weave the green strip round the birds to make branches. Pin the strip in place then slip-stitch along both edges.

PREPARATION

Cut borders 13 cm (5 in) wide in contrasting fabric, two 50 cm (20 in) long and two 90 cm (36 in) long. Stitch to the main piece of fabric (see Basic Techniques). Make card templates of the enlarged motifs and cut each one out several times from the fabric scraps.

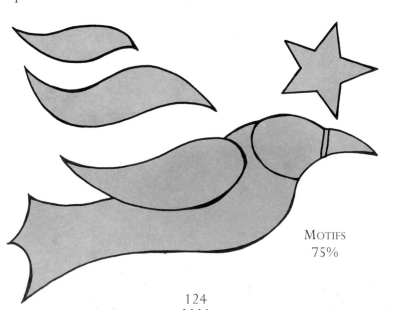

MOTIFS
75%

TO FINISH

Appliqué the leaves to the branches then fill in the spaces with stars. Sandwich the wadding (batting) between the cover and backing, right sides out, and tack (baste) through all three layers. Decorate the birds with small stab stitches. Make up the quilt (see Basic Techniques).

BABY'S APPLIQUÉ PILLOW
· · · · · ·

This little pillow is appliquéd with naïve bird and star motifs. The centre is surrounded by two borders, in gingham and striped fabric.

YOU WILL NEED
· · · · · ·

pencil and paper
iron-on interfacing
assorted fabric scraps
iron
dressmaker's scissors
36 cm x 90 cm (14 in x 36 in) calico
sewing machine and matching thread
blue and brown embroidery thread
crewel needle
small button (optional)
scraps of blue gingham
scraps of blue striped fabric
25 cm (10 in) square cushion pad
needle and matching thread

PREPARATION

Trace the motifs from the back of the book and transfer on to the interfacing. Iron to the fabric scraps and cut out. Cut out a 25 cm (10 in) square and a 36 cm (14 in) square in calico. Set the machine to zig zag and stitch the shapes on to the small calico square. Embellish with embroidery and sew on the button (optional). Cut four gingham strips 6 cm x 25 cm (2½ in x 10 in). Cut four striped strips 6 cm x 36 cm (2½ in x 14 in).

1
Right sides facing, make the gingham border, mitering the corners.

2
Pin and stitch the borders round the appliquéd square. Make up the striped border the same way and stitch round the first border. Clip the corners and press.

TO FINISH

Right sides facing, stitch the two calico squares together, leaving a small gap. Clip the corners and press. Turn right side out. Insert the pad and slip-stitch the gap.

PATCHWORK CUBE

This soft baby's toy is a perfect project for a beginner to patchwork. Experiment with a different pattern for each side of the cube.

YOU WILL NEED

7 cm x 90 cm (2¾ in x 36 in) fabric strips, in five colours

dressmaker's scissors

dressmaker's pins

sewing machine and matching thread

wadding (batting)

needle and matching thread

PREPARATION

Cut each strip into thirteen 7 cm (2¾ in) squares. Following the illustrations, arrange the squares into six blocks, cutting some to make triangles. You can use a different patchwork design for each side of the cube.

1

Using the flag method (see Basic Techniques), pin and stitch the squares together to make six square blocks.

2

Right sides facing, pin and stitch four blocks to the central one. Join the top block to one side block. Stitch the sides in pairs, leaving a small gap on the last one to turn through. Fill with wadding (batting) and slip-stitch the gap. Make a small rouleau loop and stitch to one corner.

OAK LEAF SEAT CUSHION

This appliquéd patchwork cushion is worked in sturdy contrasting colours. The leaves are outlined with rows of quilting, to raise them from the background fabric.

YOU WILL NEED

ruler and pencil

card (cardboard)

craft knife

30 cm x 90 cm (12 in x 36 in) red cotton fabric

46 cm x 90 cm (18 in x 36 in) white cotton fabric

dressmaker's scissors

vanishing marker

dressmaker's pins

needle and thread

red embroidery thread

crewel needle

sewing machine and matching thread

wadding (batting)

PREPARATION

Make a 15 cm (5½ in) square card (cardboard) template, and cut out five red squares and four white squares. Draw an oak leaf freehand on to card and cut out.

1

Trace the leaf on to scraps of red fabric. Add a 5 mm (¼ in) seam allowance and cut out. Clip the fabric back to the pencil line, and pin under the edges.

3

Run rows of red stitches, like haloes, round each leaf.

2

Tack (baste) each leaf to a white square, as shown. Appliqué the leaves in place with red embroidery thread.

TO FINISH

Using the flag method (see Basic Techniques), join the squares into a block of nine. Make two rouleau ties from a 4 cm (1½ in) wide strip of white fabric. Cut two backing pieces 42 cm x 28 cm (16½ in x 11 in), and make an envelope cushion cover (see Basic Techniques). Stitch the ties to the back corners of the cover. Stuff the cushion with wadding (batting).

HANGING HEARTS
• • • • • •

Make a heart-shaped cupboard freshener in patchwork and fill it with potpourri.

YOU WILL NEED
• • • • • •

paper and pencil

card (cardboard)

craft knife

assorted fabric scraps

dressmaker's scissors

dressmaker's pins

sewing machine and matching thread

15 cm (6 in) square backing fabric

iron

potpourri

scrap of ribbon

shirt buttons

PREPARATION

Enlarge the heart and cut out of card (cardboard). Cut out twelve 5 cm (2 in) squares from assorted fabric scraps.

33⅓%

TO FINISH

Clip the curves and press the heart. Turn right side out and fill with potpourri. Insert a ribbon loop and slip-stitch the opening closed. Decorate with shirt buttons.

1
Using the flag method (see Basic Techniques), join the squares, with 5 mm (¼ in) seams. Make a block four rows across, three rows deep.

2
Pin the heart template to the patchwork and cut out. Cut another heart from the backing fabric.

3
Right sides facing, stitch the two hearts together, leaving a small opening.

HANGING FAN

· · · · · ·

This little potpourri sachet is made from a small piece of patchwork sewn into the shape of a fan.

paper and pencil

card (cardboard)

craft knife

5 cm (2 in) square white felt

dressmaker's scissors

7 cm (2¾ in) square backing fabric

assorted fabric scraps

dressmaker's pins

needle and matching thread

coloured thread

sewing machine and matching thread

iron

potpourri

scrap of ribbon

PREPARATION

Make a card template of the fan shape. Trace on to the white felt and cut out the whole shape in backing fabric, adding a 1 cm (½ in) seam allowance. Cut the card into segments and use to cut out the individual pieces in scraps of fabric, adding a 5 mm (¼ in) seam allowance.

50%

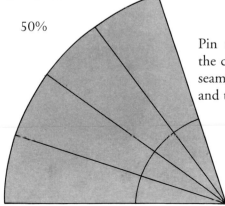

1

Pin the fabric fan shapes to the card (cardboard), fold the seam allowance over the card and tack (baste).

2

To assemble the fan shape, oversew the segments with whip stitch (see Basic Techniques). Centre the felt fan on the reverse of the patched piece and tack in place. Outline the fan segments on the right side with lines of coloured running stitches.

3

Right sides facing, stitch the patchwork piece to the backing, leaving a gap.

TO FINISH

Clip the curves and press the fan. Turn right side out and fill with potpourri. Slip-stitch the opening closed and add a ribbon loop to the top.

CHILD'S SUFFOLK PUFF WAISTCOAT
· · · · · ·

These pretty gathered rosettes are also known as bonbons and yo-yos. The Suffolk puffs are pieced together in a circle, like patchwork.

YOU WILL NEED
· · · · · ·

paper and pencil

50 cm x 90 cm (20 in x 36 in) dark print cotton fabric

pair of compasses

card (cardboard)

craft knife

scraps of pastel print, plain pastel and bright print cotton fabric

needle and matching thread

sewing machine and matching thread

pinking shears

needle and tacking (basting) thread

iron

dressmaker's pins

three buttons

matching embroidery thread

crewel needle

PREPARATION

To fit 51 cm (20 in) chest. Enlarge the waistcoat templates from the back of the book, adding a 1 cm (½ in) seam allowance. Cut out two backs and four fronts in dark print fabric. Cut an 8 cm (3 in) card (cardboard) circle. Trace 14 circles on to the assorted scraps of fabric.

1

Turn under a small hem on each fabric circle and then stitch a row of running stitches round the edges.

3

Oversew the Suffolk puffs in groups of seven to make a circle.

5

Pin and tack (baste) the Suffolk puffs to the waistcoat fronts. Using embroidery thread, work buttonhole stitch round the puffs, attaching them to the top layer (see Basic Techniques).

2

Pull up the thread tightly to gather the fabric. Secure the end of the thread. Make all the puffs in this way.

4

Stitch two waistcoat fronts to one back at the shoulders. Repeat with the other pieces to make the lining. Press the seams. Right sides facing, pin the lining to the waistcoat, matching the shoulder seams. Stitch the outer edges, leaving the side seams open, trim and clip. Turn to the right side and press. Pin and stitch the fronts to the backs at the side seams, leaving a gap to turn through. Make three buttonholes and sew on the buttons.

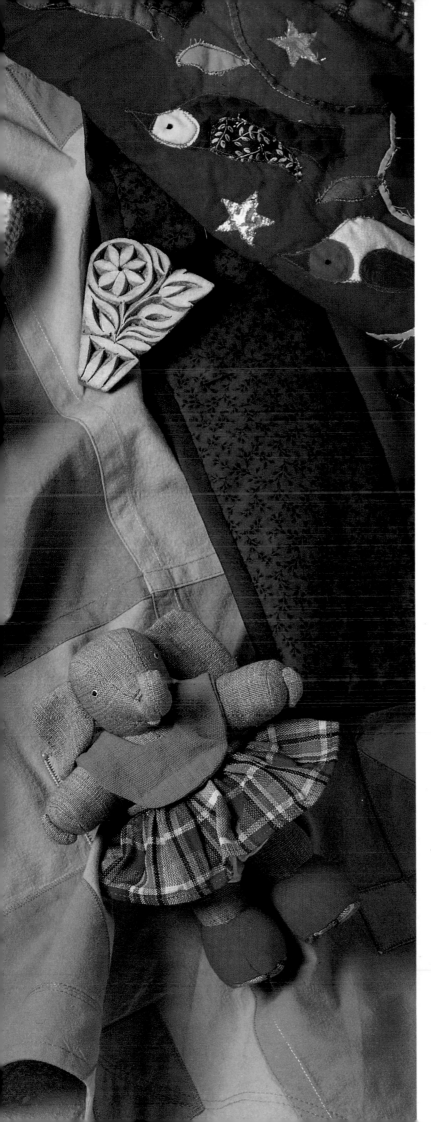

ETHNIC STYLE

Many different countries and cultures have developed stunning patchwork, quilting and appliqué designs, often quite distinct from the western tradition. There is a wealth of choice among these projects – bold geometric Seminole patchwork, folded Hawaiian appliqué, kantha quilts from Bengal, San Blas reverse appliqué, or the delicate appliqué work of the Hmong people in Vietnam and Thailand.

INTRODUCTION
······

ABOVE: A modern interpretation of the traditional Japanese kimono. Appliquéd with lustrous thread, the design is sumptuous, yet restrained.

BELOW: This beautiful modern quilt features strong patterns and colours, based on traditional Tibetan designs.

Interest in ethnic style has risen dramatically in the last 30 years. Adventurous travellers, amazed at the beauty and skill of indigenous craft objects, have brought them back to decorate their own homes. As well as being attractive souvenirs, these artifacts are steeped in local folklore. Traditions of ethnic decoration have endured the passage of time, whereas Western designs are constantly changing with the whims of fashion. The source for ethnic designs and the purpose of needlework are rooted in ancient beliefs. The decoration of textiles is extremely significant to tribal people, employing motifs which represent mythology and superstition. Potent symbols adorn embroidered and appliquéd garments, protecting the wearer from evil and bringing good fortune. Unusual talismans such as mirrors, pompons, coins and pieces of metal are used to distract and repel bad spirits.

Interest in ethnic textiles is not a new phenomenon and many traditions that have developed in the West were initiated by ideas brought over for trade and then adapted to suit Western tastes and needs. Such an example is corded quilting, which appears to have originated in the Middle East and travelled along the trade routes with merchants.

Ethnic craftspeople have in turn been influenced by Western innovations. This cross-exchange is manifested in both Hawaiian appliqué and Seminole patchwork. The Hawaiian appliqué technique evolved from a meeting of native women and American missionaries in 1820. The traditional design resembles a paper snowflake, and the fabric is folded and cut in the same way and then applied to a ground fabric. Inspiration for the designs comes from indigenous flora and fauna, and they are often quilted with stitches that echo the shape of the motif. The Seminole Indians of Florida developed their unique style of patchwork after the introduction of the sewing machine.

Appliqué has been practised worldwide for many centuries. It initially developed from a need to repair worn fabrics but it has developed into an art form in its own right. The oldest appliqué examples found are made from wool or hide date from BC. This type of appliqué is thought to have originated in the Northern hemisphere, because of its insulating properties. However, it also had a decorative element – in ancient Egypt appliqué was used to decorate funeral tents.

Indian textiles are probably the best known and loved, not only because of the country's popularity as a travel destination and the mysticism of the East, but also because of the beauty and variety of the textiles themselves. The Bengali kantha quilts have become favourite tourist souvenirs; layers of white cotton saris are decorated with motifs outlined in back stitch and filled with running stitches in red or blue thread. Imagery is drawn from the natural spirit world, with mythological beasts, animals and gods all depicted. The quilts are used as winter covers but also as wraps for precious books and objects. Appliqué hangings used as backdrops to religious gatherings and festivals have significant ceremonial importance and are usually made from silk and cotton saris. These hangings also featured reverse appliqué, in which areas of the applied fabric are cut away to reveal the layer below. The fabric to be applied is carefully folded and tacked (basted), slits are then cut into the layers and the work is opened out to reveal slightly irregular patterns. The raw edges are tucked under and slip-stitched to the ground fabric.

LEFT: A marriage of East and West. The style and fabric are definitely oriental, while the technique, shadow appliqué, is a Western invention.

The needlework techniques of the Hmong people of Laos, Vietnam and Thailand include embroidery and appliqué designs. Because of the delicacy of the work, the snipping is done while the stitching is in progress to create mazes which are derived from the patterns and rhythms of nature. The needlework is used to decorate hats, collars and the edgings of indigo-dyed jackets and trousers as well as bedcovers and cloths.

The most famous exponents of reverse appliqué are the Kuna Indian tribe of the San Blas islands, belonging to Panama. They use the technique to embellish molas, which are short-sleeved blouses. The vivid designs are eye-catching and unusual, featuring animals from Indian mythology and, oddly, political figures and slogans. This work is multi-layered, with each layer is cut away to reveal the one below. The reverse inlay technique is also used. A frame and inlay are cut to the same size in contrasting fabrics and the inlay is appliquéd to its frame. A mola is identifiable by the narrow channels, dots and sawtooth lines.

Inlay appliqué exists as a technique on its own, used when bulkiness and strength are not required, or when the design should appear on both sides, as for banners. As the raw edges butt up against each other, fabrics of the same thickness are needed. Inlay appliqué may be made in two ways – the hand-sewn method where the inlaid shape has first to be cut to fit the frame perfectly, or the machine-sewn method where two layers are assembled, the outline stitched and the top fabric cut away to reveal the shape.

This section contains a variety of projects, featuring designs and techniques from all corners of the globe. Some of the projects illustrated are lessons in traditional techniques, others are modern interpretations of ethnic themes. You may follow the projects or use the techniques for inspiration to channel into creative projects of your own. Whatever you choose you will bring something of a foreign culture and country into your life, not only in the finished item but also in the making process.

PATCHWORK DUFFEL BAG
· · · · · ·

This colourful duffel bag is made from a piece of curved block patchwork. The curved blocks bend in opposite directions when placed together for sewing.

YOU WILL NEED
· · · · · ·

50 cm (20 in) square turquoise cotton fabric

dressmaker's scissors

1 m x 90 cm (1 yd x 36 in) black cotton fabric

1 m x 90 cm (1 yd x 36 in) black lining fabric

paper and pencil

card (cardboard)

40 cm (16 in) square patterned cotton fabric

dressmaker's pins

sewing machine and matching thread

iron

80 cm (32 in) narrow piping cord

iron-on interfacing

60 cm (24 in) of 2 cm (¾ in) bias tape

needle and tacking (basting) thread

7 x 1 cm (½ in) brass rings

2 m (2 yd) thick cord

PREPARATION

The bag is made from 24 square blocks and measures 50 cm (20 in) deep by 75 cm (30 in). From the turquoise fabric, cut a top band 8 cm x 80 cm (3 in x 32 in). From the black cotton fabric, cut a circular base piece with a diameter of 30 cm (12 in), and bias strips for the piping. Cut the base to the same dimensions in the black lining fabric, then cut a lining measuring 55 cm x 85 cm (21½ in x 34 in).

TO FINISH

Tack (baste) the lining to the patchwork, wrong sides facing. Join the base to the bag and, using the narrow piping cord and the black bias strips, bind with piping (see Basic Techniques). Iron interfacing to the turquoise top band, turn under a small hem at top and bottom and pin to the bag. Insert six evenly spaced, doubled-over pieces of tape and rings round the band, and top stitch in place. Sew the last ring to the base. Thread the thick cord through the six rings and then tie it to the bottom ring.

1
Trace the three templates from the back of the book on to card (cardboard). Cut out 24 pieces in each of the fabrics, using template 1 for the black, template 2 for the patterned fabric and template 3 for the turquoise fabric. Mark the notches and clip the curves (see Basic Techniques).

2
Working from the centre out, pin three different coloured pieces together between the notches to form a block. Repeat to make 24 blocks altogether. Stitch and press each block.

3
Lay out the blocks and arrange the design, alternating the curves as shown. Using the flag method (see Basic Techniques), sew into strips of four blocks. Sew the strips together to make one large patched piece, six blocks by four blocks.

CALICO BAG

The quilted base and pockets of this calico bag make it very strong, and so an ideal choice for travelling. When not in use, store bed linen in it for the spare room. The generous pockets can be filled with soap, towels and toothbrush to welcome your guest.

YOU WILL NEED

3 m x 90 cm (3 yd x 36 in) calico

50 cm x 90 cm (20 in x 36 in) cotton corduroy

1 m (1 yd) wadding (batting)

dressmaker's scissors

vanishing marker

dressmaker's pins

needle and tacking (basting) thread

sewing machine and matching thread

7 x 1 cm (½ in) eyelets (grommets)

2 m (2 yd) cotton rope

1

Place the wadding (batting) base circle between the corduroy and calico circles and tack (baste). Machine zig zag from the centre in a spiral. Tack the pocket piece, then zig zag lines up and down it. Remove the tacking threads.

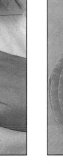

3

Pin the pocket piece and strips to the lower edge of the bag with the eyelet (grommet) positioned centrally, and hanging 4 cm (1½ in) below the lower edge. Top stitch the strips to the bag.

2

Pin and stitch the bias calico strip to the base. Stitch the short strip of calico to the longest strip, fold over the small strip by 5 cm (2 in), tack and zig zag to make a square. Attach an eyelet (grommet).

PREPARATION

For the base, cut a circle of calico, corduroy and wadding (batting) 43 cm (17 in) in diameter. For the pockets, measure the circumference of the circle and cut a piece of calico the length of the circumference by 45 cm (18 in). Fold this lengthwise round a strip of wadding (batting) and pin. For the bag, cut another piece of calico the length of the circumference by 60 cm (24 in). Cut five calico strips 8 cm x 55 cm (3 in x 21½ in), one 8 cm x 65 cm (3 in x 26 in) and one 5 cm x 8 cm (2 in x 3 in). Cut a wide bias strip to fit the circumference of the base.

TO FINISH

Turn the top of the bag to the outside, first 1 cm (½ in), then 5 cm (2 in), and then another 5 cm (2 in). Press down and top stitch. Join the base to the bag and complete the binding. Attach pairs of eyelets (grommets) to the strips at the top of the bag, and thread with the rope.

CRAZY PATCHWORK PRAM QUILT
• • • • • •

Crazy patches are a fun way to use up tiny scraps of fabric. However, like most patchwork, the best results are those which use a limited number of complementary colours and prints.

YOU WILL NEED
• • • • • •

1 m x 90 cm (1 yd x 36 in) plain cotton fabric

dressmaker's scissors

assorted cotton scraps

iron

50 cm x 90 cm (20 in x 36 in) iron-on fusible bonding web

sewing machine and matching thread

70 cm x 90 cm 28 in x 36 in) wadding (batting)

70 cm x 90 cm 28 in x 36 in) backing fabric

PREPARATION

For the sashing, cut seven plain strips 21 cm x 7 cm (8¼ in x 2¾ in), and ten 21 cm x 8.5 cm (8¼ in x 3¼ in). Make up the sashing (see Basic Techniques). From the cotton scraps, cut two patterned pieces 7 cm (2¾ in) square, four 8.5 cm (3¼ in) square, and six 7 cm x 8.5 cm (2¾ in x 3¼ in). Cut the rest of the plain cotton into six 21 cm (8¼ in) squares.

TO FINISH

Sandwich the wadding (batting) between the patched piece and the backing. Tack (baste) the layers together. Trim the wadding to the finished edge and trim the backing to 2 cm (¾ in) from the edge. Turn the backing over to the top, and mitre the corners (see Basic Techniques).

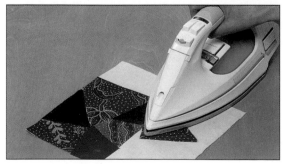

1
Iron the fusible bonding web on to the plain cotton squares and peel off the backing paper. Arrange the fabric scraps on the surface of the bonding web. Butt the edges of the scraps together and iron in place.

2
Set the machine to zig zag and stitch the scraps to the squares. Sew the squares together in horizontal rows using the flag method (see Basic Techniques). Stitch the rows together then sew to the sashing.

ETHNIC STYLE

CRIB QUILT

This pretty little quilt is made from twelve squares in an assortment of colours. It is appliquéd with naive animal and flower motifs. Choose an ethnic-inspired print for the backing fabric and motifs.

YOU WILL NEED

40 cm x 90 cm (16 in x 36 in) cream cotton fabric

20 cm x 90 cm (8 in x 36 in) green cotton fabric

20 cm x 90 cm (8 in x 36 in) yellow cotton fabric

dressmaker's scissors

card (cardboard) and pencil

craft knife

vanishing marker

scraps of iron-on fusible bonding web

iron

1 m x 90 cm (1 yd x 36 in) printed cotton fabric

sewing machine and matching thread

embroidery thread

crewel needle

1 m x 90 cm (1 yd x 36 in) calico

1 m (1 yd) wadding (batting)

PREPARATION

Cut the plain fabrics into 20 cm (8 in) squares: six cream, four green and two yellow. Enlarge the motifs and cut out in card (cardboard). Trace round the templates on to the bonding web and cut out. Iron to assorted scraps of the printed fabric and then cut out.

1
Iron the motifs to the plain cotton squares and appliqué with a machine zig zag stitch. Embellish the motifs with colourful embroidery.

FLOWER PETAL AND CENTRE 50%

ELEPHANT 50%

BIRD 50%

TO FINISH

Sew the squares together using the flag method (see Basic Techniques). Stitch horizontally into strips, then stitch the strips together. Cut the calico and wadding (batting) to the same size as the patchwork and cut the printed backing fabric 8 cm (3 in) larger all round. Bring the backing over to the front, mitre the corners (see Basic Techniques) and slip-stitch.

SAN BLAS OVEN MITTS

Layers of brightly coloured cotton are used to make these attractive oven mitts. The bird shape is cut away layer by layer, and stitched by hand to reveal a different colour each time. The designs used by the San Blas Indians usually feature birds and animals.

YOU WILL NEED

dressmaker's paper

dressmaker's scissors

90 cm x 45 cm (36 in x 18 in) red cotton fabric

90 cm x 45 cm (36 in x 18 in) blue cotton fabric

90 cm x 45 cm (36 in x 18 in) white felt

vanishing marker

40 cm x 23 cm (16 in x 9 in) yellow cotton fabric

40 cm x 23 cm (16 in x 9 in) green cotton fabric

paper and pencil

dressmaker's pins

embroidery scissors

crewel needle

red, blue and green embroidery thread

iron

25 cm x 2.5 cm (10 in x 1 in) red bias binding

PREPARATION

Cut a pattern piece in dressmaker's paper 75 cm x 18 cm (30 in x 7 in), and round off the ends. Cut one in red cotton, one in blue cotton and one in white felt. Mark the pattern piece 20 cm (8 in) from one end and cut along the marked line for the mitt. Cut out two in red, yellow and green fabric, four in blue fabric and four in white felt.

1

Layer the pattern pieces in two stacks: blue, yellow, green, blue and red. Separate the bottom blue pieces. Pin the rest together. Enlarge and trace the bird motif from the back of the book twice, reversing it the second time.

2

Cut out one paper bird motif and place it on one mitt. Draw round it in pencil. Tack (baste) an inner line, 5 mm (¼ in) from the pencil line, to show where to cut.

3

Cut away the red fabric inside the outline, leaving a small turning. Snip into the curves. Using red thread, turn under a small hem and slip-stitch through all layers.

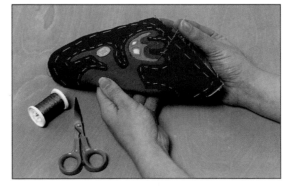

4

Draw the wings, head and tail on to the blue fabric. Cut away to reveal the green layer and hem in blue. Cut away to reveal the yellow wing details and hem in green thread. Remove the tacking stitches and press. Tack style reserved blue cotton piece to the last yellow piece as a lining. Bind the straight edge of the mitt with bias binding. Repeat for the second mitt, reversing the motif.

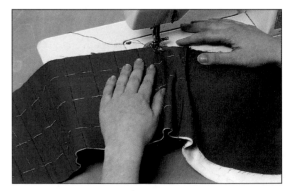

5

Tack pieces of cut felt to each end of the long felt strip. Lay this on the blue fabric with the extra felt next to the blue, and tack together. Mark a 4 cm (1½ in) grid along the length of the blue strip and machine quilt in red thread. Remove the tacking threads. Tack the red strip to the white felt. Lay the mitts with the blue lining facing the long red strip, tack and then sew close to the edge. Bind round the edges, then machine a bias binding loop to the join.

SAN BLAS CUSHION

· · · · · ·

This San Blas panel has been made up in brightly coloured cotton and sewn to a hessian (burlap) patch with a fringed border. The patch is then sewn on to a hessian cushion cover.

YOU WILL NEED

· · · · · ·

50 cm x 90 cm (20 in x 36 in) red cotton fabric

50 cm x 90 cm (20 in x 36 in) yellow cotton fabric

50 cm x 90 cm (20 in x 36 in) green cotton fabric

50 cm x 90 cm (20 in x 36 in) blue cotton fabric

dressmaker's scissors

paper and pencil

needle and tacking (basting) thread

crewel needle and yellow, blue, red, green and ecru embroidery thread

embroidery scissors

80 cm x 90 cm (32 in x 36 in) hessian (burlap)

dressmaker's pins

sewing machine and matching thread

40 cm (16 in) cushion pad

PREPARATION

Cut three red, two yellow, one green and one blue 20 cm (8 in) squares of fabric. Layer them red, yellow, green, red, yellow, blue, red, and tack (baste) together. Enlarge the motif and transfer to the fabric. Work the bird in San Blas appliqué (see San Blas Oven Mitts project). Machine a line 1 cm (½ in) from the edge of the patch and trim back. Cut out two pieces of hessian (burlap) 43 cm (17 in) square for the cover. Cut a hessian patch 28 cm (11 in) square.

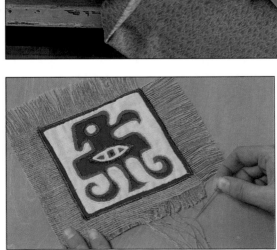

1

Pin the bird motif on to the hessian (burlap) patch. Set the machine to zig zag and work satin stitch round the edge of the patch. With a pin draw the threads along all four sides to make the fringe. Make an envelope cushion cover to fit the pad (see Basic Techniques).

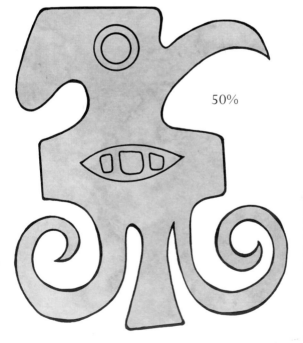

50%

SAN BLAS DRAWSTRING BAG

· · · · · · ·

Nine patches are sewn together to make the front panel for this colourful drawstring bag. The animal motifs include a butterfly, a peacock and a fish, and are taken from traditional South American designs.

YOU WILL NEED
· · · · · ·

45 cm x 71 cm (18 in x 28 in) red cotton fabric

sewing machine and red thread

25 cm x 90 cm (10 in x 36 in) red cotton fabric

25 cm x 90 cm (10 in x 36 in) yellow cotton fabric

25 cm x 90 cm (10 in x 36 in) blue cotton fabric

25 cm x 90 cm (10 in x 36 in) green cotton fabric

dressmaker's scissors

tracing paper and pencil

dressmaker's pins

crewel needle

red, yellow, blue and green embroidery thread

embroidery scissors

1 m (1 yd) thick cord

PREPARATION

To make the bag, fold over one of the long edges of the fabric by 5 cm (2 in), turn under a small hem and machine stitch. Cut the patchwork fabric into enough squares to make nine patches measuring 11 cm (4½ in) square. Layer the squares and tack (baste) together in stacks. Enlarge the motifs and transfer to the patches. Work the San Blas appliqué (see San Blas Oven Mitts project).

50%

1

Join the patches in strips of three, then join the three strips to make a square.

TO FINISH

Pin the patchwork square to one side of the red fabric, parallel to the lower edge. Set the machine to zig zag and stitch the patchwork to the bag. Right sides facing, fold the bag in half and make up (see Basic Techniques). Thread the top channel with the cord and knot the ends.

CHILD'S SAN BLAS WAISTCOAT

Here the reverse appliqué method is worked in a machine zig zag stitch to give a rich surface to two pockets, which are then used to decorate a child's waistcoat.

YOU WILL NEED

commercial waistcoat pattern to fit 61 cm (24 in) chest

50 cm x 90 cm (20 in x 36 in) red cotton fabric

50 cm x 90 cm (20 in x 36 in) yellow cotton fabric

dressmaker's scissors

25 cm (10 in) square green cotton fabric

25 cm (10 in) square blue cotton fabric

needle and tacking (basting) thread

paper and pencil

sewing machine and blue, yellow, green and red thread

embroidery scissors

crewel needle and red embroidery thread

dressmaker's pencil

PREPARATION

Cut out the waistcoat back and two fronts in both red and yellow fabric. For two pockets, cut out four red, three yellow, two green and two blue squares, each 12.5 cm (5 in) square. Trace the templates from the back of the book. For the frog, layer these blue, yellow, green, yellow, red. Tack (baste) together. For the snake, layer blue, yellow, red, green. Tack together. Enlarge the motifs on to paper and trace on to each pocket, adding a 1 cm (½ in) border.

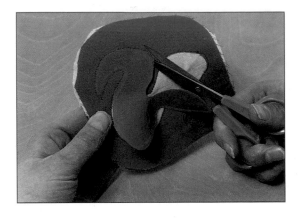

1

To make the first pocket, machine stitch a line round the frog outline in blue. Cut away inside the stitching to reveal the yellow layer.

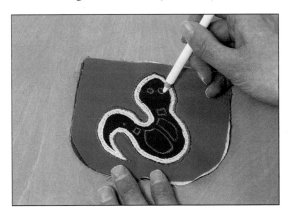

3

Draw the outline of a circle in the frog's middle and then draw on the eyes and a mouth. Stitch and cut away these to reveal yellow. Zig zag in green. Stitch a smaller circle in the middle and cut away to show the red. Zig zag in yellow.

TO FINISH

Press the pocket, turn right side out and slipstitch the gap. Make the snake pocket to match. Pin and tack (baste) the pockets to the waistcoat fronts and attach with red half-cross stitches. Make up the waistcoat following the pattern instructions.

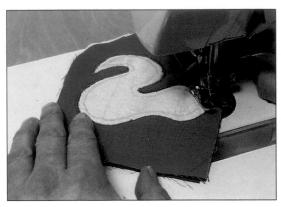

2

Zig zag stitch the raw edges in blue. Stitch inside the new outline in yellow and cut away as before to show green, then zig zag in yellow.

4

Right sides facing, stitch the red lining piece to the pocket, leaving a 5 cm (2 in) gap, and clip the curves.

POCKET TEMPLATE 50%

GREETINGS CARD
· · · · · ·

This patchwork technique is still used by the Seminole Indians to sew together strips of fabric, which are then cut into segments and re-sewn. Here paper strips are sewn together with a zig zag stitch to make a stunning design to appliqué on to a greetings card.

YOU WILL NEED
· · · · · ·

selection of coloured papers
pencil
paper scissors
sewing machine and matching thread
paper and pencil
card (cardboard)
paper varnish

75%

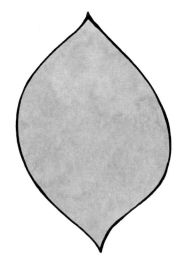

TO FINISH

Cut a piece of card (cardboard) 15 cm x 25 cm (6 in x 10 in) and fold in half widthways. Stitch the motif in place and varnish.

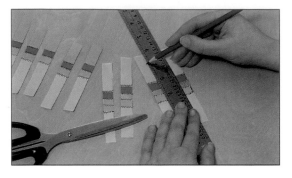

1

Measure and cut two strips of paper 3 cm (1¼ in) wide, and three strips 1 cm (½ in) wide. Arrange the three narrow strips between the two wide ones. Set the sewing machine to a medium zig zag. Overlap the strips and stitch together.

2

Cut into sections 1 cm (½ in) wide then offset the sections, matching the stitch lines so that they are staggered. Overlap and stitch together. Make two more shapes in the same way.

3

Cut two strips 3 cm (1¼ in) wide, two 1 cm (½ in) wide and a centre strip 2 cm (¾ in) wide. Arrange the narrow strips either side of the centre strip, and the wider strips outside these. Stitch and cut into 2 cm (¾ in) sections.

4

Cut 1 cm (½ in) strips. Offset and stagger the sections as before, matching the stitch lines. Insert the 1 cm (½ in) strips between the stitched sections, overlap and stitch.

5

Cut a strip across the highest and lowest points of the diamond. Arrange the narrow strip between two wide ones, overlap and stitch.

6

Enlarge the template and transfer to the patchwork piece, then cut out the motif.

NOTEBOOK COVER

This notebook has been covered with a piece of Seminole patchwork. The paper is cut on the diagonal, sewn and patched to form diamonds. Cover an address book and diary to make a matching set.

YOU WILL NEED

notebook

card (cardboard)

selection of coloured papers

pencil

craft knife

paper scissors

*sewing machine and
matching thread*

paper glue

paper varnish

PREPARATION

Open the notebook, lay it flat on a piece of card (cardboard) and draw round it. Using a ruler and craft knife, cut out the shape. Fold the card in half and press firmly along the fold line.

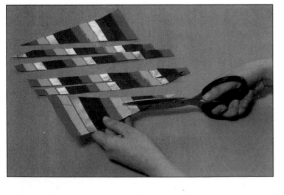

TO FINISH

Cut the patchwork into a rectangle and glue it to the piece of card (cardboard). Leave to dry and then trim to size. Varnish the cover and when dry, glue to the notebook.

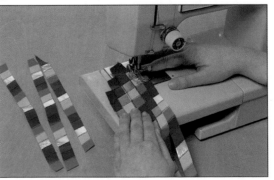

1

Measure the paper into strips 2 cm (¾ in) wide and cut out. Set the sewing machine to zig zag. Overlap the strips and stitch into one piece. Cut the piece into angled sections 2 cm (¾ in) wide, as shown.

2

Overlap the sections so that they are staggered to form vertical diamond shapes. Use up all the sections. Stitch together.

PADDED COAT HANGER

Padded coat hangers are a practical way to keep clothes in good shape. Make this piece of Seminole patchwork from satin ribbons – the end result will be very colourful.

YOU WILL NEED
• • • • • •

37 cm (15 in) wooden coat hanger

tape measure

scrap of wadding (batting)

dressmaker's scissors

needle and tacking (basting) thread

5 cm x 50 cm (2 in x 20 in) satin ribbon in three colours

sewing machine and matching thread

vanishing marker

scraps of ribbon

PREPARATION

Measure the coat hanger and cut a piece of wadding (batting) to fit. Wrap round the hanger and tack (baste) the long edges together.

TO FINISH

Wrap the metal hook with a length of ribbon and slip-stitch in place. Decorate with contrasting ribbon.

1
Machine the ribbons together. Mark across every 5 cm (2 in) and cut into strips.

2
Arrange the strips, offsetting them so that they are staggered. Reverse every other strip. Make two patches of equal length. Right sides facing, stitch them together round the edges, leaving a gap on the top edge.

3
Turn right side out and cover the hanger. Turn under a hem on the raw edges and slip-stitch.

GIFT TAGS
• • • • • •

These gift tags are made from patchwork strips cut from plain coloured paper. Patterned gift wrapping paper could also be used in the same way to make an interesting piece of Seminole patchwork.

YOU WILL NEED
• • • • • •

selection of coloured papers

paper scissors

sewing machine and matching thread

card (cardboard)

paper glue

paper varnish

hole punch

scraps of ribbon

DESIGN A PREPARATION

Cut two strips of paper in one colour 2 cm (¾ in) wide and one contrasting strip 1 cm (½ in) wide. Arrange the narrow strip between the wide ones. Overlap and machine zig zag stitch together. Next cut two strips 2 cm (¾ in) wide in two different colours, and one strip in a third colour 1 cm (½ in) wide. Arrange and stitch as before.

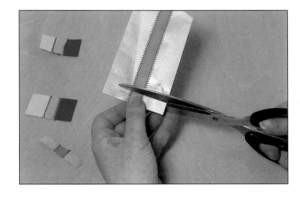

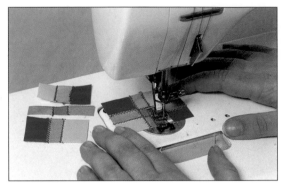

1
Cut the first patch into strips 1 cm (½ in) wide, and the second into strips 2 cm (¾ in) wide.

2
Arrange as shown, with one narrow strip placed between two wide ones, then stitch.

DESIGN B PREPARATION

Cut two strips of paper in two different colours 2 cm (¾ in) wide, and two strips in two more colours 1 cm (½ in) wide. Arrange the narrow strips between the wide ones. Overlap and machine zig zag stitch together. Next cut three strips of paper in different colours, one 3 cm (1¼ in), one 2 cm (¾ in) and one 1 cm (½ in) wide. Stitch the narrow strip between the two wide ones.

TO FINISH

Cut two pieces of card (cardboard) to size and glue on to the paper patches. Varnish and leave to dry. Punch a hole in one corner of each card and thread with ribbon.

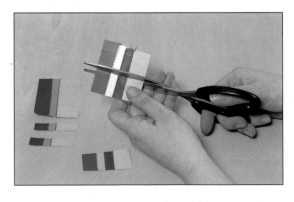

1
Cut one patch into strips 2 cm (¾ in) wide, and one into strips 1 cm (½ in) wide.

2
Arrange as shown, with two narrow strips placed between two wide ones, then stitch.

SASHIKO QUILT

Sashiko quilting originated in Japan in the 18th century as protective clothing worn by firemen. The wadding (batting) is held between two layers of indigo fabric with white running stitches – the closer the stitches, the more durable the garment.

YOU WILL NEED

card (cardboard}

pencil

craft knife

2 m x 90 cm (2¼ yd x 36 in) assorted plain and print cotton fabrics

dressmaker's scissors

1.3 m x 1.6 m (52 in x 64 in) wadding (batting)

sewing machine and matching thread

iron

dressmaker's pins

1.3 m x 1.6 m (52 in x 64 in) cotton backing

vanishing marker

white quilting thread

crewel needle

PREPARATION

Make three card (cardboard) templates, one 11 cm (4½ in) square, one 5 cm (2 in) square and one 3 cm (1¼ in) square. Using the 11 cm (4½ in) template, cut the plain and print fabrics into 180 squares.

1

Using the two smaller card templates, draw three squares on each plain fabric square – two diagonal to the fabric square, and repeat the smallest square as a square on top of the smallest diagonal.

2

Lay the squares 12 across and 15 down. Stitch in horizontal rows using the flag method (see Basic Techniques). Press the seams in opposite directions. Stitch the strips together.

3

Sandwich the wadding (batting) between the patched piece and the cotton backing. Pin and tack (baste) the layers together (see Basic Techniques). Quilt along the marked lines in white thread using running stitch.

TO FINISH

Trim the wadding (batting) back to the finished edge and trim the backing to 2 cm (¾ in) from the edge. Turn the backing over to the top, mitre the corners and slip-stitch.

SASHIKO BAG
· · · · · ·

A small piece of sashiko quilting is easy to transform into an envelope bag. First make the quilted square then follow the instructions to make the bag.

YOU WILL NEED
· · · · · ·

2 m x 90 cm (2 yd x 36 in) blue cotton fabric

dressmaker's scissors

vanishing marker

1 m (1 yd) square wadding (batting)

needle and tacking (basting) thread

white quilting thread

crewel needle

embroidery scissors

sewing machine and matching thread

4 m (4 yd) pink bias binding

bead or button

PREPARATION

Cut the blue fabric into two pieces 1 m (1 yd) square. Mark a 75 cm (30 in) square in the centre of one blue square. Mark a diamond pattern to fill the central square. Sandwich the wadding (batting) between the two cotton squares and tack (baste), first round the edges then working from the middle out.

1
Work a row of running stitches in quilting thread diagonally across the marked square. Work the diamond pattern, making the same number of stitches in each section. At the intersections, miss a stitch.

2
Work tiny running stitches in rows of parallel lines round the borders.

3
Machine stitch the binding to the wrong side round the edges. Pull the four corners together and stitch two seams with the binding sandwiched between, facing the right side. Fold over binding on the remaining sides and top stitch. Fasten the bag with a thread loop and a bead or button.

PATCHWORK CURTAIN

Checked and appliquéd patches are arranged diagonally in a checker board design for this curtain.
Choose a bold, ethnic design to complete the look.

YOU WILL NEED

tape measure

*dyed calico, in two colours
(see Preparation below)*

dressmaker's scissors

*50 cm x 90 cm (20 in x
36 in) iron-on interfacing*

dressmaker's pins

*sewing machine and
matching thread*

paper and pencil

*scraps of cotton fabric, for
the appliqué*

needle and thread

*curtain tape, to fit the curtain
width plus 2.5 cm (1 in)*

curtain hooks

PREPARATION

To calculate how much fabric
you will need, measure the
window and multiply by
three. For the drop, add an
extra 10 cm (4 in) to the
length. Cut some calico in
one colour into 30 cm (12 in)
squares. Arrange them on the
floor checker board style to
the size of the curtain. Cut a
few squares diagonally in half
to make triangles for the
edges. Cut the interfacing into
30 cm (12 in) squares. Then
cut 10 cm (4 in) squares in
both calico colours, and
arrange and pin groups of nine
squares to the interfacing. Zig
zag stitch over the raw edges.
Make enough checked squares
to complete the curtain.

1

Draw a bold, ethnic-inspired design on paper,
or copy ours from the picture. Cut out each
shape in fabric scraps and iron interfacing on
to the back. Pin to the plain calico squares.

2

Tack (baste), then appliqué each shape with
machine zig zag stitch on to the plain calico
squares to secure in place.

TO FINISH

Using the flag method (see
Basic Techniques), join the
squares in strips then join the
strips. Turn a small machine
hem on both long sides of the
curtain. Press the top under
1 cm (½ in) and, with wrong
sides facing, tack (baste) on
the curtain tape. Stitch. Turn
under a hem on the bottom
edge and slip-stitch. Attach
the curtain hooks. Repeat if
you wish to make a pair of
curtains.

CURTAIN TIE-BACKS

Complete your window dressing with a pair of striking tie-backs based on the shape of a man's tie!
Decorate them with bias strips of fabric sewn in stripes.

PREPARATION

To make a template, draw round the tie, squaring off the narrow end and adding 2.5 cm (1 in) to the other three sides. Cut out four pieces in the main colour. For the appliqué stripes, cut strips in both contrasting colours on the bias, 3 cm (1¼ in), 5 cm (2 in) and 6 cm (2½ in) wide.

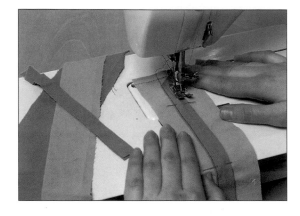

1

Join the bias strips on the wrong side, following the main picture for guidance. Trim and press the seams.

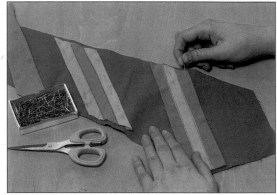

2

Iron interfacing to the back of the strips. Press under a turning then lay the strips on the tie shape. Pin, tack (baste) and machine stitch.

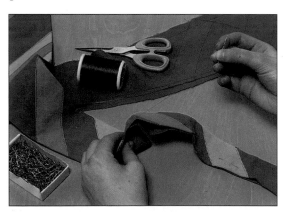

3

Right sides facing, place the patchwork shape on a plain tie shape. Stitch round the edge, leaving a small gap. Clip, press and pull through. Slip-stitch the opening. Make the second tie-back the same way.

4

Attach the brass rings. Roll up 24 cm (9½ in) from the narrow end of the tie-backs and stitch down by hand.

BOLSTER CUSHION
· · · · · ·

This small bolster cushion is made from calico and ribbed silk. A pattern of slashes is cut into the top silk fabric and neatly hemmed to the calico under-cover. This creates the interesting texture, which is complemented by fringing.

YOU WILL NEED
· · · · · ·

paper and pencil

*70 cm x 90 cm
(28 in x 36 in) calico*

*70 cm x 90 cm
(28 in x 36 in) raw silk*

dressmaker's scissors

vanishing marker

sharp scissors

iron

*needle and tacking
(basting) thread*

*sewing machine and
matching thread*

wadding (batting)

PREPARATION

Cut a paper template for the main piece. Cut out in both calico and silk. For the base, cut two in each fabric. To make the frayed fringe, cut two strips of calico, 5 cm x 55 cm (2 in x 21½ in).

TO FINISH

Right sides facing, stitch the short ends to make a tube, leaving a 10 cm (4 in) gap in the middle for turning. Tack (baste) the fringe strips each end of the tube. Stitch the base pieces to the tube. Turn the bolster right side out and fray the calico down to the seam line using a needle. Fill the bolster with wadding (batting) and slip-stitch the opening closed.

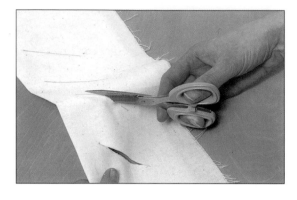

1

Transfer the slash line design to the calico with a vanishing marker and cut with sharp scissors.

2

Turn under a small hem on each of the slash lines and press on to the wrong side. Tack (baste) the calico to the silk round the almond shapes.

3

Slip-stitch round the almond shapes. Press flat on the wrong side.

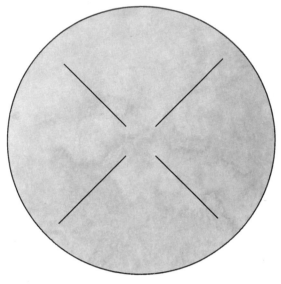

BASE
18 cm (7 in)

MAIN PIECE

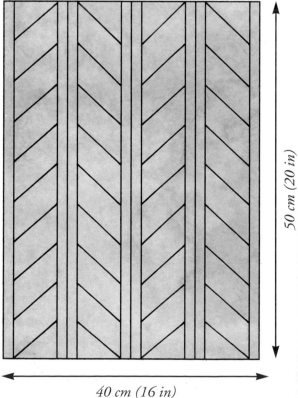

50 cm (20 in)

40 cm (16 in)

BOOK COVER

· · · · ·

Inlay appliqué is worked in silk to make this luxurious book cover. Rectangles are cut into the top layer and patches of brightly coloured silks are then fitted into the frame.

YOU WILL NEED
· · · · · ·

book

black silk scrap to fit the book, plus 5 cm (2 in)

vanishing marker

dressmaker's scissors

orange silk scrap, twice the size of the black silk

needle and tacking (basting) thread

sharp scissors

dressmaker's pins

matching thread

assorted silk scraps in bright colours

sewing machine

PREPARATION

Open the book, lay it flat on the black silk and draw round it. Cut out with a 2.5 cm (1 in) seam allowance. Cut another piece in orange silk. Halve the remaining piece of orange silk, lay the closed book on it, draw the outline and cut two pieces plus seam allowances.

TO FINISH

To make the cover pockets, turn under a hem on the long edge on each orange half piece. Machine stitch in place. Right sides facing, pin to the book cover and stitch. Fit the book sleeves into the pockets.

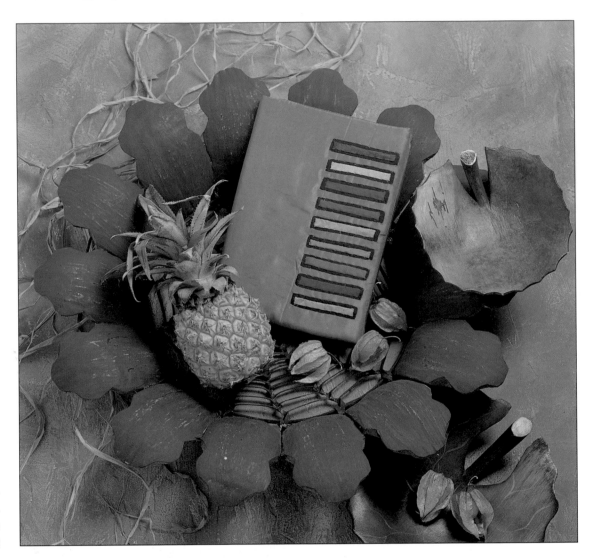

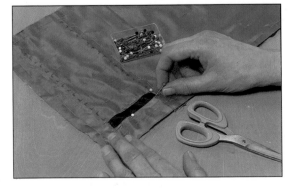

1

Tack (baste) the large piece of orange silk on top of the black silk. Mark a row of rectangles down the centre front half. Tack through the marked lines. One rectangle at a time, cut into the corners through the top layer. Turn under a hem round the rectangle, pin and stitch.

2

Cut several pieces of silk in assorted colours to fit the black rectangles. Centre and tack each piece in the centre of one black rectangle on the right side. Hem the inlay piece and push it behind the frame. Slip-stitch to the black silk.

SLASHED SILK BAG

This intriguing little box is made from patches of slashed silks, sewn together inside out. This makes a design feature out of the seams and the ragged texture. The box is fastened with a silk loop and a knotted silk button.

YOU WILL NEED

25 cm x 90 cm (10 in x 36 in) calico

dressmaker's scissors

iron

15 cm x 90 cm (6 in x 36 in) iron-on interfacing

scraps of silk in six contrasting colours

dressmaker's pins

sewing machine and matching thread

embroidery scissors

PREPARATION

Cut ten 12.5 cm (5 in) calico squares. Iron the interfacing to the squares and place them in pairs, interfacing sides together. Cover each one with six assorted silk squares cut to the same size and pin.

1

Stitch a line 1 cm (½ in) round the edges of each square then stitch lines, 1 cm (½ in) apart, within the square. Slice between the lines, cutting through all the colours except the last.

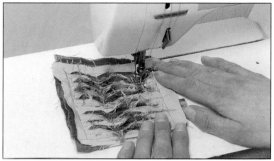

2

The layers of fabric will escape to the surface. Stitch a horizontal line across the vertical cuts in one direction, then work back in the other direction, 1 cm (½ in) apart. Cover the whole area in this way.

3

Place two finished squares together, calico sides facing, and stitch 1 cm (½ in) from the edge. Stitch another decorated patch to each side of the central square.

TO FINISH

Stitch the sides of the bag together. Sew a silk loop and a knotted button made from silk scraps to the top.

APPLIQUÉ FELT BALL
· · · · · ·

This soft ball is safe to play with and big enough for a baby to hold easily. It is decorated with colourful appliqué shapes worked in simple embroidery stitches.

YOU WILL NEED
· · · · · ·

paper and pencil
card (cardboard)
craft knife
20 cm x 90 cm
(8 in x 36 in) calico
dressmaker's scissors
scraps of coloured felt
dressmaker's pins
embroidery hoop
assorted embroidery threads
crewel needle
needle and matching thread
wadding (batting)
scrap of ribbon, optional

PREPARATION

Trace the pentagon and make 12 templates in thin card (cardboard). Draw 12 pentagons on the calico, spacing them at least 2.5 cm (1 in) apart, but do not cut out. Make heart and petal templates and cut out in coloured felt. Cut two sizes of small circles for the flower centres.

1

Pin a circle and heart to one pentagon. Place the calico in the embroidery hoop. Work a running stitch round the heart. Stitch an asterisk to hold the circle in place. Appliqué all the pentagons in this way.

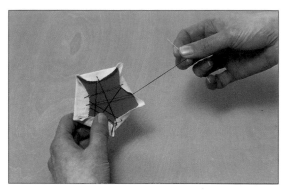

2

Cut out the pentagons, adding a 1 cm (½ in) seam allowance. Stretch the calico patches over the templates (see Basic Techniques).

3

Whip stitch five patches to one central patch to make half a ball. Repeat for the second half.

4

Stitch the two halves together, leaving three seams unsewn. Remove the templates.

TO FINISH

Fill with wadding (batting) and close the last seams. If you wish, insert a small ribbon loop into the last seam to hang the ball.

HEART

PENTAGON

PETAL

BABY BLANKET

. . . . . .

This is another example of inlaid appliqué. Here the method is used to stitch a bird motif on to a baby's blanket. The motif is then decorated with brightly coloured embroidery threads.

YOU WILL NEED
. . . . . .

wool blanket

dressmaker's scissors

paper and pencil

card (cardboard)

craft knife

scraps of coloured blanket fabric

dressmaker's pins

vanishing marker

needle and tacking (basting) thread

sharp scissors

sewing machine and contrasting thread

iron

assorted embroidery threads

crewel needle

PREPARATION

Cut the blanket to the required size for a cot (crib) or child's bed. Enlarge and trace the bird motif and cut templates in card (cardboard). Cut out the shapes in coloured fabric, adding a 2 cm (¾ in) seam allowance. Position the templates on the right side of the blanket and draw round. Tack (baste) carefully over the line.

1

Pin and tack the bird shapes to the wrong side of the blanket, on top of the tacked outline.

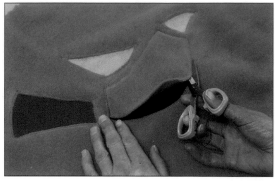

2

From the right side, carefully cut the fabric along the outline.

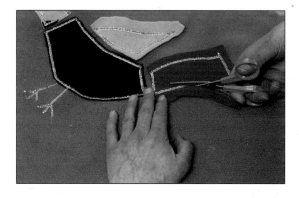

3

Set the machine to zig zag, pin a piece of paper to the wrong side of the appliqué pieces and work a wide satin stitch over the raw edges. Stitch the bird's legs, as shown. Trim away any excess fabric.

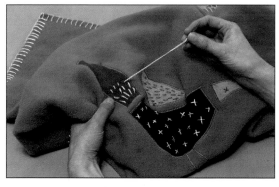

4

Press under a narrow hem all round the blanket and stitch with a wide blanket stitch in contrasting thread. Hand stitch details on to the bird using embroidery threads.

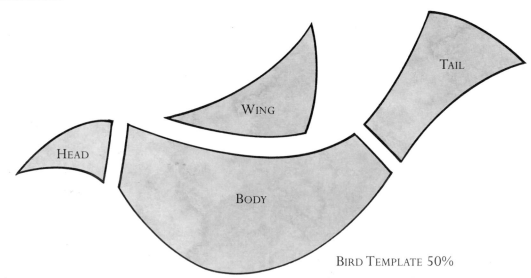

TAIL

WING

HEAD

BODY

BIRD TEMPLATE 50%

SEMINOLE TOWEL

• • • • • •

A geometric patchwork piece, cut into narrow strips then stitched in rows, makes an attractive border for a bathroom towel.

12 cm x 90 cm (5 in x 36 in) cotton fabric in two colours

vanishing marker

dressmaker's scissors

iron

scrap of iron-on fusible bonding web

sewing machine and matching thread

20 cm x 90 cm (8 in x 36 in) backing fabric

dressmaker's pins

bath towel

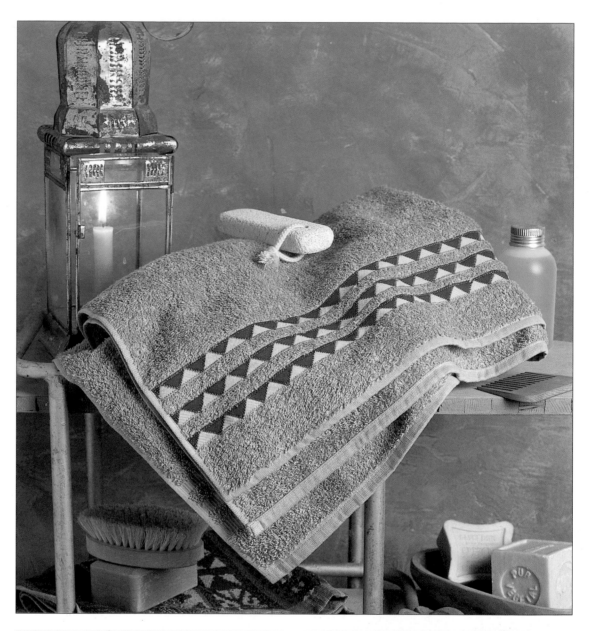

PREPARATION

Cut both cotton fabrics into three strips 6 cm x 40 cm (2½ in x 16 in), and iron to the bonding web. Alternate the colours so that the strips overlap. Machine together with a zig zag stitch to make one piece of patchwork.

1

Cut the patchwork into strips 2 cm (¾ in) wide. Offset the strips on a piece of backing fabric as shown and iron on. Secure with a zig zag stitch.

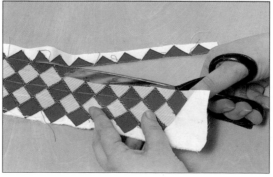

2

Mark a horizontal line through the centre of the diamonds and cut into long strips.

3

Pin several strips to each end of the towel, running parallel to the edge. Machine in place.

QUILTED EGG COSY

This egg cosy is a tiny copy of a traditional Nepalese hat. It is quilted in cotton fabric with white thread and topped with a woollen tassel.

YOU WILL NEED

card (cardboard) and pencil

craft knife

dressmaker's scissors

18 cm x 24 cm (7 in x 9½ in) plain cotton fabric

18 cm x 24 cm (7 in x 9½ in) lining fabric, in contrasting colour

15 cm x 20 cm (6 in x 8 in) wadding (batting)

needle and tacking (basting) thread

vanishing marker

white quilting thread

crewel needle

embroidery scissors

sewing machine and matching thread

scraps of knitting wool

PREPARATION

Enlarge the template and cut out in card (cardboard). Cut out two pieces in both cotton and lining, adding a 1 cm (½ in) seam allowance all round. Cut out two pieces in wadding (batting), without any seam allowance, and sandwich each between the cotton and the lining. Tack (baste) the layers together (see Basic Techniques). Mark a geometric design, in freehand, on to both cotton shapes.

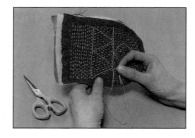

1

Work over the design in small, neat running stitches with quilting thread, filling the whole area. Make the second side the same.

2

Trim the top fabric back to the wadding. Bind the lower edge with lining fabric and top-stitch. Right sides facing, stitch round the seam line.

3

Cut a piece of card (cardboard) 1 cm x 2.5 cm (½ in x 1 in) and wind lengths of knitting wool round it several times. The more you wind, the thicker the tassel.

50%

TO FINISH

Pull the wool carefully off the card (cardboard) and secure at the top with a short length of wool. Splice the wool through the other end of the loop, and trim. Bind the uncut strands together at the top. Stitch the tassel to the top of the finished egg cosy.

PA NDAU APPLIQUÉ FRAME

An elaborate maze design from the Hmong people of South East Asia, known as "crooked road" or "frog's legs". This normally complicated appliqué technique is simplified here.

YOU WILL NEED

dressmaker's scissors

45 cm x 90 cm (18 in x 36 in) black cotton fabric

30 cm x 60 cm (12 in x 24 in) white cotton fabric

45 cm (18 in) square graph paper

pencil

thick black pen

spray starch

iron

vanishing marker

dressmaker's pins

needle and matching thread

embroidery scissors

two mount board squares, 17.5 cm (6¾ in) square and 16.5 cm (6½ in) square

double-sided tape

fabric glue

brass curtain ring

PREPARATION

Cut the black fabric in half to make two pieces 45 cm (18 in) square, and the white fabric to make two pieces 30 cm (12 in) square.

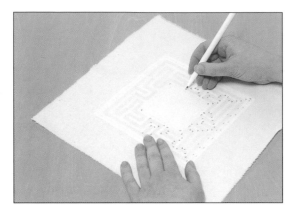

1

Trace the template from the back of the book on to graph paper and fill in the lines of the design with thick black pen. Spray both sides of one white square with starch and press. Lay the fabric on top of the graph paper and mark the corners of the design with the vanishing marker.

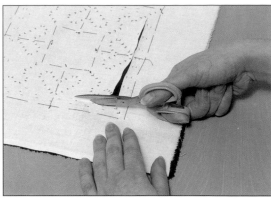

2

Place one square of black cotton between the two white squares with the marked one uppermost. Pin and tack (baste) around the inside and outside edges of the fabric frame. Tack (baste) crossways in the middle of each side. Cutting one section at a time, make a slit in the outside black line, always keeping the line central. Snip into the corners.

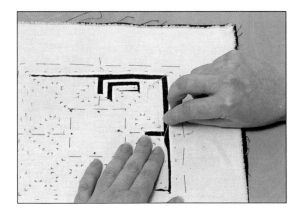

3

Using the point of the needle, fold under a tiny turning and slip-stitch a hem. Stitch closer together at the corners. Work the whole frame one quarter at a time. Use the corner marks as guidelines and keep referring back to the original design.

4

Pin a small hem on the outside and inside edges of the finished piece. Cut a 6 cm (2½ in) square in the centre of the large mount board. Lay the appliqué face down and cut into the corners of the window. Stretch the white fabric on to double-sided tape. Glue the black fabric to cover the small square. Place together and slip-stitch the sides. Sew a brass ring to the top.

PA NDAU APPLIQUÉ BOX LID

· · · · · ·

Another simplified design from the Hmong tribes, created with a stencil. Enlarge the design if you
want to cover a different-sized box.

YOU WILL NEED
· · · · · ·

*25 cm x 50 cm (10 in x
20 in) red cotton fabric*

dressmaker's scissors

paper and pencil

paper scissors

*wooden box, 14 cm
(5½ in) square*

spray starch

iron

*25 cm (10 in) square yellow
cotton fabric*

vanishing marker

embroidery scissors

needle and matching thread

*14 cm (5½ in) square
wadding (batting)*

fabric glue

double-sided tape

corded red ribbon

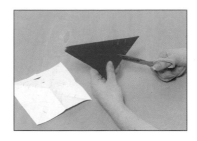

1

Cut the red fabric into two
pieces 25 cm (10 in) square.
Cut a square of paper to fit
the lid. Halve diagonally, and
then halve again. Trace the
design. Snip into each line,
open out to check the pattern
and then refold the stencil.

2

Starch one red fabric square.
Fold diagonally to match the
paper and press. Using the
paper stencil, mark in the
lines. Working from the
centre outwards, snip into the
fabric as with the paper.
Unfold the fabric and press.

3

Place the cut fabric on to the
yellow and red squares. Tack
(baste) 1 cm (½ in) away from
the snipped fabric. Cut along
the lines between snips,
cutting two lines at a time.
Turn a small hem on the
outside edge. Snip into the V's
at the inner edge, turn a hem
and slip-stitch.

4

Draw four 5 mm (¼ in)
quarter circles in the centre of
the appliqué. Snip into the
corners, turn under a small
hem and slip-stitch. Remove
any remaining tacking stitches
and press.

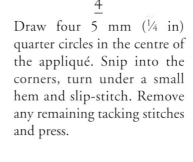

5

Glue the wadding (batting) to
the lid, and stick tape round
the top of the box. Trim the
appliqué to 16 cm (6¼ in),
stretch over the lid and on to
the tape. Mitre the corners
and stick more tape to the
sides. Glue red ribbon on top
to finish.

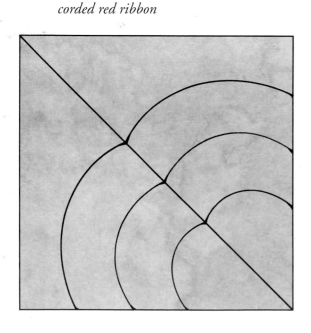

CALICO NAPKIN

· · · · · ·

This homemade napkin is appliquéd and stitched by hand. Alternatively, appliqué the simple motif on to ready-made napkins.

YOU WILL NEED
· · · · · ·

card (cardboard) and pencil

craft knife

fabric scraps in blue, pink, cream and green

dressmaker's scissors

48 cm (19 in) square calico

tailor's chalk

scrap of iron-on fusible bonding web

iron

dressmaker's pins

green and blue embroidery thread

crewel needle

PREPARATION

Enlarge the heart motif and make a card (cardboard) template. Cut out in blue fabric, adding a 1 cm (½ in) seam allowance. Press under a small hem on the heart and the calico square. Draw the flower and leaves freehand on to the bonding web and cut out. Iron the shapes on to the scraps. Cut out, pin and iron on to the heart.

1

Embroider a green stalk and randomly appliqué the shapes on to the heart. Pin and appliqué the heart to a corner of the napkin.

2

Fill the heart with running stitches then finish the edges of the napkin with a decorative running stitch border.

50%

TABLE MATS

· · · · · ·

These simple table mats look particularly effective if made in a rough-textured cotton fabric. They are decorated with fringed edges and simple running stitches worked in colourful threads, which hold the wadding (batting) in place.

YOU WILL NEED
· · · · · ·

2 m x 90 cm (2¼ yd x 36 in) checked cotton fabric

dressmaker's scissors

1 m (1 yd) wadding (batting)

needle and tacking (basting) thread

assorted embroidery threads

crewel needle

sewing machine and matching thread

iron

PREPARATION

Cut the fabric into eight pieces, each measuring 50 cm x 45 cm (20 in x 18 in). Cut the wadding (batting) into four pieces 40 cm x 36 cm (16 in x 14 in). Sandwich the wadding between two pieces of fabric, leaving a 5 cm (2 in) overlap on all sides. Tack (baste) one piece of fabric to the wadding, then turn over and repeat with the second piece of fabric.

TO FINISH

Press the mats flat and trim any stray threads.

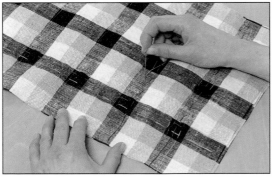

1
Work rows of running stitch in parallel lines right across the mat. Sew through all the layers, changing colours as you go. Remove the tacking (basting) threads.

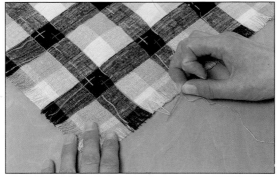

2
Machine stitch a line round the mat, 5 cm (2 in) from the raw edges. With a needle, pull threads to fringe the edges. Repeat for the other three mats.

WOOL HAT
· · · · · ·

This hat with a turn-back border is made from blanket fabric, and ties in a knot at the crown. The inlaid appliqué motifs which run round the border are whip stitched in a contrasting colour.

YOU WILL NEED
· · · · · ·

*40 cm x 90 cm
(16 in x 36 in) woollen
blanket fabric*

dressmaker's scissors

paper and pencil

card (cardboard)

craft knife

vanishing marker

*scraps of woollen blanket
fabric in two colours*

*60 cm x 5 cm (24 in x 2 in)
iron-on interfacing*

iron

needle and contrasting thread

*sewing machine and
matching thread*

PREPARATION

Cut a piece of fabric 60 cm x 40 cm (24 in x 16 in). Turn under a double hem, 2 cm (¾ in) wide, and machine stitch. Cut two ties 23 cm x 5 cm (9 in x 2 in). Trace and cut templates out of card (cardboard).

1
Alternate the two templates along the hem, drawing round them. Cut out the shapes.

2
Draw the shapes on to the wool scraps, and cut out an equal number in each colour. Lay a cut motif into a corresponding shape and iron the interfacing over it. Work along the hem fusing the interfacing to the fabric as you go.

3
Right sides facing, whip stitch over the cut edges in a contrasting colour (see Basic Techniques). Fold the hat in half and machine the top and back seams.

4
To make the ties, press under both long and one short edge, fold in half lengthways and zig zag round the edges. Slip the raw ends into each top corner of the hat. Turn back the appliquéd border and slip-stitch to the hat. Stitch the ties to the top seam and tie in a knot.

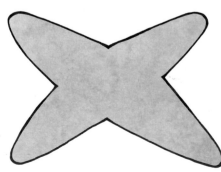

BABY'S APPLIQUÉD CARDIGAN
· · · · · ·

Felt animal motifs reminiscent of mola work are appliquéd with tiny blanket stitches in a contrasting colour. Knit this patchwork cardigan, or buy one ready-made.

YOU WILL NEED
· · · · · ·

3 x 25 g (1 oz) balls random-dyed red yarn

1 x 25 g (1 oz) ball in two contrasting shades

4 mm (No 8) knitting needles

white, red and navy felt

dressmaker's scissors

needle and tacking (basting) thread

paper and pencil

embroidery scissors

dressmaker's pins

white, red and navy embroidery thread

crewel needle

TO FIT: 50 cm (20 in) chest
ACTUAL SIZE: 58 cm (23 in)
LENGTH: 29 cm (11½ in)
SLEEVE LENGTH: 23 cm (9 in)

PREPARATION

Tension: worked in stocking stitch on 4 mm (No 8) needles, 20 sts x 24 rows measures 10 cm (4 in). Knit the cardigan as follows.
Back: knit a piece 52 sts wide by 32 cm (13 in) long, with a 1 cm (½ in) border and divided into 16 patches, each 13 sts wide by 7 cm (2¾ in) deep.
Fronts: cast on 26 sts and work in patches, as back. Knit straight to 15 cm (6 in). Shape the neck by decreasing 9 sts on one edge over the remaining rows. Reverse the shapings for the other front.
Sleeves: cast on 39 sts and work a 2 cm (¾ in) border. The sleeves are divided into nine patches. Press lightly. Sew the shoulder seams and set in the sleeves. Sew the side and sleeve seams.
Cut the felt into 10 cm (4 in) squares and layer red/white/red or navy/white/navy and tack (baste). Cut one stack for each front and each sleeve.

<u>1</u>

Trace the motifs from the back of the book on to paper and then transfer to felt. Cut out the felt shapes, cutting a wide base layer, and cut eyes and mouth from the top layer. Pin and tack (baste) the first shape to the cardigan. Working in layers, secure with small blanket stitches in contrasting coloured threads.

<u>2</u>

For the fastenings, cut four 2.5 cm (1 in) squares in white felt and fold in half to make triangles. Place the straight folded edge to the front edge of the cardigan and pin. Blanket stitch round two sides of the triangle in red.

<u>3</u>

For each tie, cut three 28 cm (11 in) lengths of embroidery thread. Sew the threads to the front, under the felt triangles. Plait the threads and tie together.

CHILD'S PATCHWORK SWEATER
· · · · · ·

This sweater is made of strips of different coloured squares knitted with simple motifs. The strips are then sewn together into blocks. The finished seams are laced in white and the border edged with pompons.

YOU WILL NEED
· · · · · ·

1 x 25 g (1 oz) ball yarn in six shades

4 mm (No 8) knitting needles

pencil and squared paper

needle and matching thread

small amount of white yarn

crewel needle

70 cm (28 in) pompon tape

TO FIT: 61 cm (24 in) chest
ACTUAL SIZE: 68.5 cm (27 in)
LENGTH: 33 cm (13 in)
SLEEVE LENGTH: 23 cm (9 in)

PREPARATION

Tension: Worked in pattern on 4 mm (No 8) needles, 24 sts x 26 rows measures 10 cm (4 in). To obtain the correct tension, change the needle size.

Draw the motifs from the back of the book on to squared paper. Each block is 26 stitches by 28 rows. For the back and front, knit three strips of three blocks. Shape the front neck half way up the last centre block.

1
For each sleeve, knit two strips of two blocks. Pin and sew the strips together from the wrong side.

2
Lace the work on the right side over the joined seams using white yarn. Then lace across from left to right to separate the coloured blocks.

3
Neaten the edges by knitting two rows round the neck edge and lower sleeve edges. Sew the pompon tape round the bottom edge.

APPLIQUÉ SUNFLOWER
· · · · · ·

Appliqué a shiny satin flower on to the bib of a child's dress or dungarees (overalls). This simple motif is stitched by hand.

YOU WILL NEED
· · · · · ·

paper and pencil

card (cardboard)

craft knife

scraps of iron-on interfacing

sharp scissors

iron

assorted satin scraps

dressmaker's pins

needle and matching thread

PREPARATION

Copy the templates on to card (cardboard) and cut out. Transfer each petal and the flower centre on to the interfacing. Cut out the shapes with a sharp pair of scissors.

1
Iron the interfacing shapes to the back of the satin scraps. Cut out, adding a 5 mm (¼ in) seam allowance.

2
Turn under a hem on the raw edges, pin and tack (baste).

3
Position the motif on the garment. Pin and slip-stitch each section in place.

FLOWER CENTRE AND PETAL

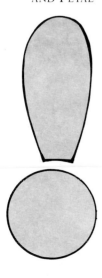

KANTHA QUILT

· · · · · ·

This traditional method of echo quilting is used in India. Complex quilting patterns are formed by echoing the shapes of patchwork or appliqué motifs with a halo of tiny stitches, worked in two or more parallel lines.

YOU WILL NEED
· · · · · ·

paper and pencil

card (cardboard)

craft knife

dressmaker's scissors

70 cm x 90 cm (28 in x 36 in) wadding (batting)

70 cm x 90 cm (28 in x 36 in) muslin

1 m x 90 cm (1 yd x 36 in) backing fabric

needle and tacking (basting) thread

vanishing marker

assorted embroidery threads

crewel needle

sewing machine and matching thread

PREPARATION

Enlarge the templates and cut out of card (cardboard). Sandwich the wadding (batting) between the muslin and backing fabric and tack (baste). Mark a border 11 cm (4½ in) from the edges with a row of tacking stitches.

TO FINISH

Trim the muslin and the wadding (batting) by 2 cm (¾ in), then bring the backing fabric over to the top and bind the raw edges (see Basic Techniques).

<u>1</u>

Trace the paisley and bird motifs on to the quilt border. Find the centre of the quilt and draw a flower freehand, then trace the elephants in the centre square.

<u>2</u>

Work a neat back stitch round the outline of all the motifs using red embroidery thread.

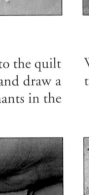

<u>3</u>

Work tiny running stitches inside each motif in various colours to echo the outline.

<u>4</u>

Using thread that matches the quilt, work tiny running stitches in a halo round each motif to echo the shapes filling the whole quilt.

PEACOCK AND PAISLEY 50%

ELEPHANT 50%

HAWAIIAN APPLIQUÉ HANGING

Patchwork and appliqué were taken to Hawaii by missionaries in the 19th century, but it was the Hawaiians themselves who developed this unique method of appliqué. The motifs are folded and cut in the same way as paper snowflakes.

YOU WILL NEED
• • • • •

*1 m x 90 cm (1 yd x 36 in)
green cotton fabric*

*43 cm (17 in) square
cream cotton fabric*

dressmaker's scissors

spray starch

iron

30 cm (12 in) squared paper

pencil

paper scissors

vanishing marker

needle and matching thread

embroidery scissors

*46 cm (18 in) square
wadding (batting)*

dressmaker's pins

embroidery hoop

quilting thread

crewel needle

PREPARATION

Cut the green cotton into two 43 cm (17 in) squares and a 10 cm (4 in) strip. Spray starch both sides of one green square and press. Cut three 10 cm (4 in) wide strips of fabric, fold the loops in half and stitch. Turn right side out. Enlarge the design from the back of the book.

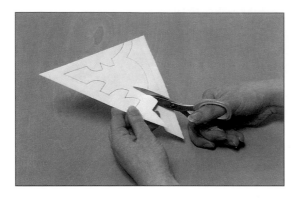

1

Fold the paper into quarters and then fold again into a triangle. Trace the design on to the triangle. Draw the border round the edge following the shape of the snowflake. Cut along the lines and open out.

3

Cut the green fabric a little at a time to 3 mm (⅛ in) from the pencil line. Snip the curves.

5

Sandwich the wadding (batting) between the appliquéd square and the green cotton, securing the loops. Pin and tack.

2

Trace round the template on to the green square using the vanishing marker and tack (baste) to the cream square, 5 mm (¼ in) from the outline of the motif and 5 mm (¼ in) from the outline of the border.

4

Press on the wrong side. Neaten the edges, turning under a small hem. Slip-stitch in place.

TO FINISH

Stretch the appliqué on an embroidery hoop. Starting at the edge, hand quilt halos round the snowflake. Work parallel rows of tiny running stitches round the border. Trim the edges of the square. Cut two strips of green fabric 10 cm x 38 cm (4 in x 15 in), and two strips 10 cm x 46 cm (4 in x 18 in). Stitch to the edges as borders (see Basic Techniques).

POTPOURRI CUSHION
· · · · · ·

Appliqué a scrap of fabric, Hawaiian style, on to an organza cushion and fill with sweet-smelling potpourri. Decorate with old linen buttons and use as an air freshener or relaxing pillow.

YOU WILL NEED
· · · · · ·

paper and pencil

20 cm (8 in) square organza fabric in two colours

dressmaker's scissors

needle and tacking (basting) thread

vanishing marker

embroidery hoop

sewing machine and matching thread

sharp scissors

potpourri

linen buttons

PREPARATION

Cut a piece of paper 16 cm (6¼ in) square. Fold in half, and in half again. Fold one corner to its opposite, and draw on the motif. Cut out. Tack (baste) the two squares of organza together. Position the paper template and transfer the motif.

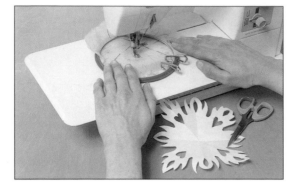

1
Centre the organza in the embroidery hoop. Set the machine to darning mode, and work a straight stitch all round the marked outline.

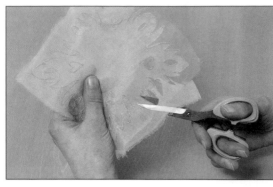

2
Trim away the excess top fabric. Work several more lines of stitching over the first, to cover the raw edge fully.

TO FINISH

Tack (baste) together the two remaining organza squares, and place them right sides facing the appliquéd piece. Make up the cushion (see Basic Techniques). Fill with potpourri and slip-stitch to close. Decorate the edges with linen buttons.

BEADED PURSE

· · · · · ·

This purse is appliquéd with fabric hearts which are embellished with beads and coloured threads. It fastens at the top with a loop and button.

YOU WILL NEED

12 cm x 32 cm (4 ¾ in x 13 in) blue fabric

dressmaker's scissors

12 cm x 32 cm (4 ¾ in x 13 in) red lining fabric

scraps of fabric for the hearts

scraps of iron-on interfacing

iron

embroidery hoop

needle and matching thread

assorted beads

sewing machine and matching thread

wooden button

red embroidery thread

PREPARATION

Fold the long ends of the blue fabric together and cut in half. Repeat with the red lining. Cut four large and four small contrasting hearts from the scraps and iron interfacing on to the back.

1

Using an embroidery hoop, appliqué two large hearts on to each blue square then appliqué two small hearts on top. Embellish with beads and decorative stitching. Right sides facing, machine stitch together.

2

Make a red lining and attach to the purse. Sew the button to the top of the purse. Plait six strands of embroidery thread, 20 cm (8 in) long, and tie with a knot. Stitch the plait to the back of the purse in a loop.

• • • • • •

CONTEMPORARY STYLE

• • • • • •

Create your own modern versions of these traditional crafts with contemporary fabrics such as PVC and bright colour schemes. To update a design repeated on a large quilt, focus on a single appliqué motif or patchwork block and feature it on a child's bag or a cushion. Don't be afraid of being bold or adventurous, but follow in the spirit of the first quiltmakers who used whatever materials they could find to make original works of art.

INTRODUCTION

ABOVE: This delightful sea-inspired appliqué picture is full of contemporary style.

Textile crafts are constantly changing and evolving to fit the moods of fashion. After a decline in popularity, patchwork and appliqué were revived in the 1960s and '70s, together with interest in ethnic textiles and a fascination for the American pioneer lifestyle. During these two decades, patchwork garments were embroidered with motifs and sentimental or political slogans, in a similar fashion to the crazy patchwork quilts of the Victorian era.

The projects in this section update the textile traditions of the past. The colours and patterns are bold and dramatic, the motifs quirky and modern. Instructions are given for contemporary items such as rucksacks and T shirts, as well as modern interpretations of traditional items. For speed and convenience, block designs are used as single motifs and simplified for machine sewing. Mosaic patchwork, which is usually made up of hundreds of geometric shapes, has been re-designed and the patches enlarged to save time. Patches must be cut with exactly measured seam allowances for machine-sewn patchwork – accuracy is essential to ensure that all the shapes fit and the seams are aligned.

Using a sewing machine imposes certain constraints on patchwork design. Many-sided shapes are difficult to piece and joining curved seams is not easy. Smaller shapes are fiddly to work with and a diagonal patch will need careful stitching to prevent distortion. Iron-on interfacing, cut to the size of the finished patch and used as a backing, will not only stabilize the fabric but also serve as a guide for machine-stitching. The easiest shape to fit is a square or rectangle; these can be stitched into strips, and then the strips joined. For a beginner, the square is the ideal shape. Select two contrasting shades to create a bold checker board effect. Advanced needleworkers might like to design their own geometric patchwork, as it is, after all, a highly personal craft. Contemporary patchworkers have often been influenced by geometric

RIGHT: Hand-made paper is not the first appliqué material to spring to mind, but it can be utilized to produce beautiful contemporary items, such as this paper portfolio.

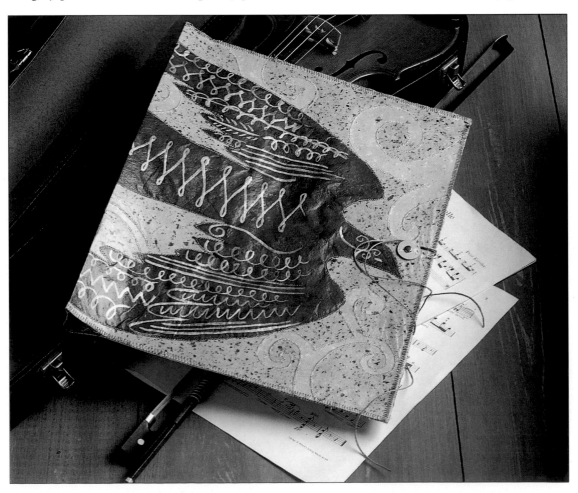

patterns found in other forms of decoration. Islamic architecture is particularly interesting for its colourful mosaics, stained glass and cut stone designs.

In these days of mass production, the desire to personalize textiles is strong, and there is a great deal of pleasure to be found in designing and making, and satisfaction in the completion of the work. Perhaps the most important consideration is that of time. We no longer wish to spend long hours on one item – most of us would prefer to start and finish a project in one day. Thankfully, developments in specialist materials and equipment help to minimize the time spent in preparation.

Iron-on fusible bonding web has revolutionized the art of appliqué. The immediacy of this method is extremely attractive, with the interfacing bonding one layer of fabric to another. Bonding agents, such as pastes and starches, have been used for many years, but the modern version is much simpler to use. Its main advantage is that it prevents fabric from puckering, fraying or shifting before or during stitching. As the interfacing is paper-backed, motifs can be easily traced on to it before application. It also lines the fabric, so a light fabric applied to a dark ground will not show through. Usually appliqué edges are neatened with a narrow machine satin stitch, but if the appliquéd item will only receive light wear then they may be hand-stitched. For really quick results, leave the edges of motifs unstitched and use pinking shears to prevent the edges from fraying.

Cotton fabrics are traditionally chosen for textile projects and are certainly the easiest to use. Select firmly woven fabric, and do not choose cottons with a high manmade content as they will not press well. Cotton fabrics are easy to wash, and are available in many colours and prints. More skilled needleworkers may be more adventurous. Contemporary textile artists use a variety of exciting fabrics such as PVC, plastics (acetates) and organza woven in silk and metallic fibres. For patchwork, you must use fabrics of equal weight, but for appliqué you can use almost any combination of weights. Other materials, such as paper and fur fabrics give texture, and you can recycle old woollen garments to make felt. Another short cut is to use felt as an appliqué fabric, as it non-woven and therefore does not fray. Felt is ideal for items that do not need laundering. Knitted or stretch fabrics are not suitable for appliqué or patchwork projects.

Seek out interesting trimmings, beads, sequins, buttons and ribbons to add detail to a piece. Specialist manufacturers also produce a variety of machine and hand embroidery threads, including neons and metallics. With the advances in synthetic dyes, there are an incredible range of shades.

ABOVE: A cot quilt with a folk motif, this is still a very up-to-date interpretation.

BELOW: Patchwork and appliqué techniques may be ages old, but the choice of fabrics and materials dictates this contemporary style.

PEG BAG

· · · · · ·

This peg bag is made from patchwork triangles placed in alternating colours to look like a windmill. Choose a contrasting piece of printed fabric to make up the bag.

YOU WILL NEED

· · · · ·

40 cm x 90 cm (16 in x 36 in) printed cotton fabric

dressmaker's scissors

paper and pencil

card (cardboard)

craft knife

1 m x 90 cm (1 yd x 36 in) green cotton fabric

50 cm x 90 cm (20 in x 36 in) yellow cotton fabric

dressmaker's pins

sewing machine and zipper foot

matching thread

1 m x 90 cm (1 yd x 36 in) piping cord

37 cm (15 in) wooden coat hanger

PREPARATION

Enlarge the diagram from the back of the book on to paper and cut out two sides, one top and one back in printed fabric, adding a 1 cm (½ in) seam allowance. Enlarge the triangle motif and make a card (cardboard) template. Cut four triangles in green, and four in yellow, adding a 5mm (¼ in) seam allowance. To make the piping, cut a 8 cm x 65 cm (3 in x 26 in) bias strip from yellow fabric (see Basic Techniques). Join it into a circle and press the seam open.

1

Join the triangles, alternating the colours as shown, to form a square patch. Clip and press the seams to one side.

2

Right sides facing, machine the patch to the side pieces. Press the seams open. Attach the top piece the same way, trim and press the seams flat towards the top.

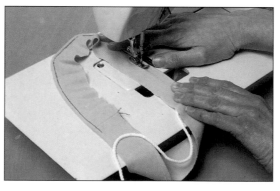

3

Fold the piping strip lengthways. Attach the zipper foot and stitch, enclosing the piping cord. Tack (baste) the piping strip to the opening, with the sewing line matching the seam. Stitch and clip the curved edge. Press under the piping seam allowance, trim and slip-stitch.

4

Right sides facing, match the front to the back, then stitch round the edge of the bag.

TO FINISH

Clip the corners, turn right side out and press flat. Push the hanger wire through the centre top seam.

PVC RUCKSACK

This rucksack is especially useful because the straps are in a luminous yellow. They will double up as safety strips on dark, winter evenings when your child is travelling home from school.

YOU WILL NEED
• • • • • •

paper and pencil

card (cardboard)

craft knife

50 cm x 90 cm (20 in x 36 in) blue PVC

50 cm x 90 cm (20 in x 36 in) yellow PVC

10 cm x 90 cm (4 in x 36 in) red PVC

dressmaker's scissors

1 m x 90 cm (1 yd x 36 in) lining fabric

dressmaker's pins

132 cm (52 in) of 4 cm (1½ in) black tape

sewing machine and matching thread

needle and tacking (basting) thread

7 large eyelets (grommets)

hammer

1 m (1 yd) nylon cord

PREPARATION

Enlarge the diagram and cut out the triangles, adding a 5 mm (¼ in) seam allowance. Follow the illustration for colour reference. Cut out a 66 cm x 32.5 cm (26 in x 12¾ in) rectangle in blue PVC for the bag. Cut out a 33 cm x 14 cm (13 in x 5½ in) rectangle in yellow PVC for the base. For the straps, cut two 7 cm x 66 cm (2½ in x 26 in) strips of yellow PVC. Cut out a bag piece and base in lining.

1

Pin and stitch the blue and yellow triangles together, following the diagram.

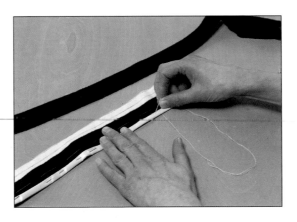

3

Cut the black tape in half and tack (baste) to the yellow PVC strips. Fold the PVC over the tape, leaving a 5 mm (¼ in) channel either side. Turn under a small hem, tack and top stitch in place. Pin the straps to the bag. Stitch the back seam, then pin and stitch the yellow base to the bag. Make up the lining, stitch along the top edge of the bag, leaving a gap. Pull through and slip-stitch the gap.

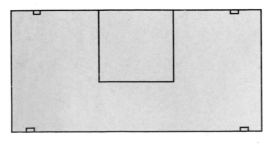

RUCKSACK PLAN 10%

2

Add the red triangles, and then the large yellow triangles. Appliqué the patch to the blue PVC bag front.

4

Attach the eyelets (grommets) 3 cm (1¼ in) from the outside top edge, spacing them evenly apart. Thread with the nylon cord and knot the ends.

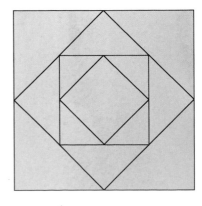

PATCH DIAGRAM 50%

CHILD'S BERET

This PVC beret with a colourful daisy appliqué will brighten up a rainy day. Alternatively, buy a ready-made beret and sew the daisy motif on to it.

YOU WILL NEED

paper and pencil

paper scissors

tracing paper

dressmaker's scissors

10 cm x 90 cm (4 in x 36 in) iron-on interfacing

iron

assorted scraps of fabric

50 cm x 90 cm (20 in x 36 in) red PVC

50 cm x 90 cm (20 in x 36 in) polka dot cotton fabric

dressmaker's pins

embroidery thread

crewel needle

sewing machine and matching thread

PREPARATION

Enlarge the templates and cut out in paper. Draw the daisy shapes on to tracing paper and transfer to the interfacing. Cut out the shapes, iron to the fabric scraps and cut out. Cut a circle in red PVC measuring 40 cm (16 in), and one in polka dot cotton for the lining. Cut a hat band, 5 cm (2 in) wide and 4 cm (1¾ in) larger than the head measurement, in both fabrics.

1

Position the daisy in the centre of the red PVC circle. Pin and blanket stitch in place, then add diagonal stitches on either side.

2

Join the short ends of the hat bands, trim and clip. Place the red PVC and the lining together, wrong sides facing, and pleat at the back of the beret. Pin the pleats, and adjust to the size of the bands.

3

Stitch the PVC band to the pleated circle, then sew the second band to the first. Trim the seams and press flat. Fold the band to the wrong side and stitch.

25%

SCOTTIE DOG T SHIRT

Decorate a plain T shirt with this Scottie dog motif. Alternatively, appliqué the motif on to a pair of dungarees (overalls).

YOU WILL NEED
......

iron
iron-on fusible bonding web
fabric scrap
paper and pencil
dressmaker's scissors
child's T shirt
needle and matching thread
13 cm (5 in) tartan ribbon
glass bead
embroidery thread

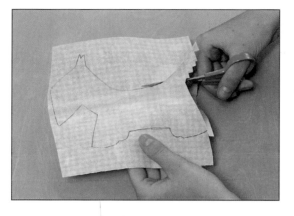

1

Iron the bonding web to the reverse of the fabric scrap. Enlarge the template and draw it on to the bonding web. Cut out the dog.

2

Peel off the backing, position the dog and iron in place. Slip-stitch to the T shirt.

3

Tie the ribbon into a bow and stitch to the dog's neck. Stitch on the bead for the eye, and work a few stitches for the mouth.

50%

BEACH BAG

• • • • • •

This clever bag opens out flat to double up as a beach mat. Ten fabric fish and the sea are sandwiched between two sheets of clear plastic.

YOU WILL NEED
• • • • • •

2 m x 90 cm (2¼ yd x 36 in) strong clear plastic

dressmaker's scissors

66 cm square (26 in) square blue satin fabric

paper and pencil

paper scissors

iron-on fusible bonding web

iron

assorted fabric scraps

marker pen

sewing machine and matching thread

1 m (1 yd) of 2 cm (¾ in) white tape

1 m (1 yd) of 2 cm (¾ in) red tape

3.5 m (3¾ yd) white bias binding

3 m (3¼ yd) thick cord

PREPARATION

Cut out two plastic circles, 90 cm (36 in) in diameter, and cut one satin circle with wavy sides, 60 cm (24 in) in diameter. Trace the fish motifs from the back of the book, varying the sizes, and cut out in paper.

1
Trace ten fish on to the bonding web. Cut out and iron on to the fabric scraps. Peel off the backing paper and iron the fish to the blue satin. Draw on the fins and eyes with the marker pen.

2
Sandwich the satin between the plastic circles and machine zig zag round the wavy outline. Cut each tape into six loops and pin round the edge. Bind the edge with bias binding. Thread the cord through the loops and knot the ends.

BEACH TOWEL

· · · · · ·

Old bath sheets or a length of towelling can be cut down to make an attractive beach towel when appliquéd with bold seaside motifs.

YOU WILL NEED
· · · · · ·

paper and pencil

paper scissors

assorted scraps of cotton fabric

iron

dressmaker's scissors

old towel or towelling fabric

sewing machine and matching thread

vanishing marker

dressmaker's pins

PREPARATION

Enlarge the seaside motifs from the back of the book and cut out in paper. Using a contrasting colour to the towel, cut two strips of fabric 1 m x 7.5 cm (1 yd x 3 in) for the binding. Turn the long edges under by 1 cm (½ in). Press.

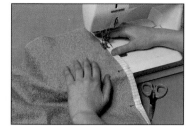

1
Pin and machine the binding to the ends of the towel or towelling fabric, enclosing the raw edges.

2
Pin the paper templates on to the fabric scraps and cut out the shapes.

3
Position and pin the motifs along one end of the towel. Overlap the bucket and spade motifs. Set the machine to zig zag and stitch in place.

BLACK-AND-WHITE APPLIQUÉ COVER

This striking design plays on positive and negative images. The design is cut out in black and white, and then appliquéd on to the reverse squares.

YOU WILL NEED
• • • • • •

3 cm (12½ in) square card (cardboard) and pencil

craft knife

1.5 m x 115 cm (1½ yd x 45 in) calico fabric

dressmaker's scissors

2 m x 115 cm (2¼ yd x 45 in) black cotton fabric

102 cm x 90 cm (40 in x 36 in) iron-on fusible bonding web

iron

sewing machine and black thread

PREPARATION

Enlarge the template on to the card and cut round the outline. Cut 12 calico and six black cotton 32 cm (12½ in) squares. Cut the bonding web into six 32 cm (12½ in) squares. Cut a backing piece in black cotton 98 cm x 1.3 m (39 in x 52 in).

1
Draw round the template on to each of the bonding web squares.

2
Iron the bonding web to the reverse of the black squares and carefully cut out the design.

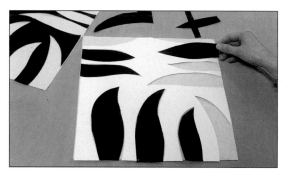

3
Peel off the backing papers and arrange the pieces from each black square on to two calico squares. Use the template as a guide for positioning the individual black pieces. Iron on.

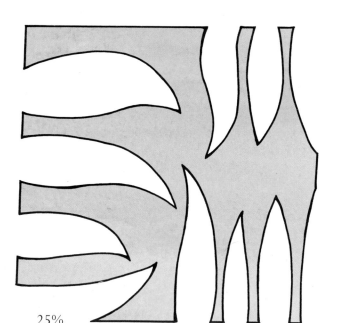

25%

TO FINISH

Using the flag method (see Basic Techniques), stitch the 12 squares into blocks of three. Stitch the blocks into four rows. Wrong sides facing, tack the cover to the backing piece. Bring the backing over to the front, mitre the corners (see Basic Techniques) and top stitch to the cover.

4
Set the machine to zig zag and stitch round the black shapes.

SCATTER CUSHIONS

This set of four cushions is made from a piece of patched fabric, which is cut up and re-sewn several times. This method of Seminole patchwork is a clever way to juggle plain fabrics to make a unique and bold design.

YOU WILL NEED

1 m x 115 cm (1 yd x 45 in) red backing silk

3 m (3¼ yd) piping cord

dressmaker's scissors

sewing machine and matching thread

38 cm (15 in) square raw silk, in four colours

iron-on fusible bonding web

iron

4 x 20 cm (8 in) cushion pads

PREPARATION

Using the red silk, make a red bias strip 3 cm (1¼ in) wide and use to cover the piping (see Basic Techniques). Cut the four squares of silk diagonally in half. Take one triangle of each colour and join to make a four-coloured square patch. Fold the square in half in both directions, and press along the fold lines.

1
Cut the fabric along the fold lines to make four small squares.

2
Cut each small square into three strips to make 12 rectangles.

3
Randomly join two sets of three strips. Halve the remaining six strips, mix and then rejoin to make six new strips. Arrange, then stitch all of the pieces to make two rectangular blocks.

4
Cut each block in half and trim the edges.

TO FINISH

Cut four 23 cm (9 in) backing squares in red silk. Right sides facing, stitch one to each of the patchwork squares, with the piping sandwiched between (see Basic Techniques). Stitch the seams, leaving a 13 cm (5 in) gap. Clip the corners, press and turn to the right side. Insert the cushion pads in each cushion and slipstitch the gap.

5
Iron the bonding web to scraps of red silk. Draw 20 circles and cut out. Peel off the backing and iron the circles on to the patches. Zig zag round the shapes in matching thread.

SILK CHRISTMAS CARDS

• • • • • •

These Christmas trees are made from strips of checked silk sewn together and cut into triangles. This simple patchwork technique is very effective.

YOU WILL NEED
• • • • • •

pencil and ruler

assorted scraps of checked silk fabric

dressmaker's scissors

sewing machine and contrasting thread

dressmaker's pins

fabric glue

card (cardboard)

paper scissors

1

Cut the silk into strips 2.5 cm x 36 cm (1 in x 14 in). Overlap the strips and then stitch together lengthways using a contrasting thread.

2

Cut the patchwork piece into triangular shapes. Using a pin, draw threads from the raw edges to fringe each layer.

3

Glue each triangle to a piece of silk backing fabric, then glue to a piece of card and cut out. Cut pieces of card (cardboard) and fold in half to make cards. Glue the trees on to the front of each card.

JAM JAR COVER

Appliqué this juicy strawberry on to a jam jar cover and embellish it with a few embroidery stitches.
Make more covers and appliqué with a variety of fruits.

YOU WILL NEED

pencil

saucer

scraps of pink and green fabric

dressmaker's scissors

iron-on fusible bonding web

iron

tracing paper and pencil

embroidery thread

crewel needle

sewing machine and matching thread

40 cm (16 in) pink ribbon

PREPARATION

Draw round a saucer on to both the pink and green fabrics and cut out two circles. Iron the bonding web on to scraps of fabric. Trace the strawberry motif on to paper, transfer on to the bonding web and cut out. Peel off the backing, centre the motif on the green fabric and iron on.

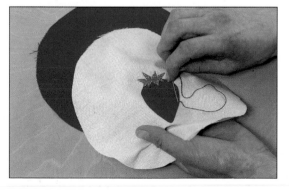

<u>1</u>

Outline the strawberry with colourful stitches. Embellish with cross stitches. Right sides facing, machine stitch the circles together, leaving a small gap.

<u>2</u>

Turn right side out. Sew running stitch round the edge. Attach the ribbon 5 cm (2 in) from the edge, place on a jam jar and tie in a bow.

APPLIQUÉ GLASSES CASE

· · · · · ·

By throwing old woollen knitwear into the washing machine, you can create a fabric with the flexibility
of wool and the texture of felt. Draw motifs of your choice freehand and
appliqué on to a glasses case.

YOU WILL NEED
· · · · · ·

paper and pencil

paper scissors

assorted scraps of felted knitting

dressmaker's scissors

20 cm x 90 cm (8 in x 36 in) silk lining fabric

dressmaker's pins

sewing machine and matching thread

20 cm (8 in) braid

50 cm (½ yd) cord

PREPARATION

Enlarge the case template on to paper. Cut out a felted cover and a lining, plus four different-
coloured felt squares to fit the cover.

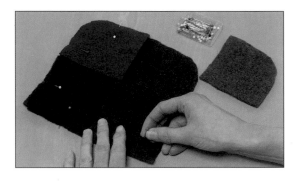

1
Pin and sew the four felt squares on to the felted cover.

2
Cut out your selected motifs in felted scraps. Arrange them on the squares and pin.

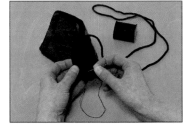

3
Machine zig zag round the edges of the motifs.

4
Right sides facing, fold the case in half lengthways and stitch the seam. Turn right side out. Bind the top edge with the braid. Stitch the cord to the top.

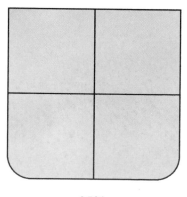

25%

JEWELLERY ROLL
. . . . . .

This jewellery roll has been machine quilted in a meandering filling stitch. Filling patterns can be used to cover the whole area or to fill in a background. They can be as simple or as complex as you wish.

YOU WILL NEED
. . . . . .

20 cm x 90 cm (8 in x 36 in) checked silk fabric

dressmaker's scissors

scrap of wadding (batting)

needle and tacking (basting) thread

sewing machine and thread

1m (1 yd) bias binding

2 press studs (snap fasteners)

dressmaker's pins

zipper foot

15 cm (6 in) zip (zipper)

button

PREPARATION

Cut two pieces of silk and one piece of wadding (batting) 18 cm x 40 cm (7 in x 16 in). Sandwich the wadding between the two pieces of silk, with the silk right side out. Tack (baste) together, starting in the middle. Cut two 23 cm (9 in) lengths of bias binding and stitch together to make one wide strip. Cut in half, turn under the ends and stitch. Sew a press stud (snap fastener) to each end.

TO FINISH

Roll up the case and mark the centre of the long edge. Sew on a button and button loop.

1
Attach the darning foot to the machine and fill the whole quilted silk piece with a meandering filling stitch – a continuous wavy line. Use a contrasting coloured thread, or pick out one of the colours in the fabric.

2
Attach ordinary bias binding to the short ends. Fold the edges over by 7.5 cm (3 in) and tack (baste). Pin the zip (zipper) to one bound edge and stitch. Stitch the other side of the zip to the case. Divide the other pocket into three with vertical stitch lines.

3
Pin the wide strip of bias binding across the middle of the case. Pin strips of bias binding to the long ends of the case, and stitch. Trim the edges, fold the binding to the right side, and top stitch.

TORAN HANGING

Designed to hang over a door, traditional torans can be found throughout India, adorning temple doorways. They are characterized by their use of brilliant colours and zany patterns as seen in this patchwork and appliqué toran.

YOU WILL NEED

paper and pencil

calico

dressmaker's scissors

wadding (batting)

assorted fabric scraps in silk, satin, velvet and cotton

embroidery scissors

embroidery hoop

assorted embroidery threads

crewel needle

beads, sequins and buttons

quilting thread

needle and tacking (basting) thread

sewing machine and thread

assorted bias binding, ribbon and tapes

curtain hooks

PREPARATION

Decide on the size and shape of your hanging and draw a plan dividing the area into patches. Cut out the shape in calico, adding a seam allowance. Cut the same shape in wadding (batting) without a seam allowance.

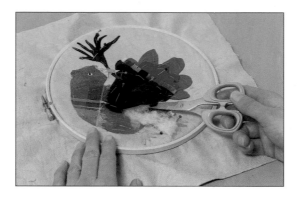

1

Cut fabric shapes freehand to form the design, then pin and tack (baste) to a fabric patch. Place in an embroidery hoop. Fill with wadding (batting) for a raised effect where necessary. Hand quilt round the shapes, stitching through all the layers. Embellish with beads, sequins and buttons.

2

Make a border from shaped patches of fabric, as shown. Right sides facing, pin along the top of the hanging. Machine stitch.

3

Fold back the border. Stitch rows of ribbon and tape along the edge of the hanging to cover the border. Pin bias binding or ribbon round the raw edges of the border. Stitch in place.

TO FINISH

Following your plan, stitch the patches together to make the toran. Sandwich the wadding (batting) between the patched piece and the calico backing, right sides out. Pin and tack (baste). Stitch a line round the outside edge. Bind any raw edges, using bias strip binding, ribbon or tape. Sew curtain hooks evenly spaced along the top edge.

1950s' BISTRO PLACEMAT

This placemat has been appliquéd with a retro design of garden vegetables. This kitsch style is typical of kitchen design in the 1950s.

YOU WILL NEED

paper and pencil

paper scissors

dressmaker's pins

red, orange and yellow fabric scraps

dressmaker's scissors

20 cm x 50 cm (8 in x 20 in) green-and-red striped fabric

10 cm x 27 cm (4 in x 10½ in) yellow gingham fabric

needle and tacking (basting) thread

vanishing marker

green and brown embroidery thread

crewel needle

sewing machine and matching thread

iron

5 cm x 36 cm (2 in x 14 in) red cotton fabric

30 cm x 36 cm (12 in x 14 in) green gingham fabric

33 cm x 42 cm (13 in x 16½ in) single-sided quilted backing fabric

PREPARATION

Enlarge the motifs from the back of the book and cut out paper templates. Pin to the scraps and cut out, adding a 5 mm (¼ in) seam allowance. Cut two green-and-red striped fabric strips 5.5 cm x 9 cm (2¼ in x 3½ in), and one 7 cm x 36 cm (2¾ in x 14 in).

1

Clip and turn under the seam allowances on the fabric motifs and tack (baste). Cut three 10 cm x 9 cm (4 in x 3½ in) rectangles from the yellow gingham fabric.

2

Tack one vegetable to each rectangle and slip-stitch in place. Mark details with a vanishing marker. Hand stitch with embroidery thread.

3

Right sides facing, stitch the two short striped strips between the appliquéd patches and press flat. Then stitch the red strip to the left edge and the long green-and-red striped strip to the right edge.

4

Right sides facing, stitch the green gingham to the red strip. Stitch one short end of the quilted fabric to the long striped strip. Tack the top to the backing. Trim the mat to 32 cm x 42 cm (13 in x 16½ in). Cut the remaining striped fabric into strips and bind the other three edges.

APPLIQUÉ BOOK COVER

Personalize a notebook with this fabric cover. Felt is a good choice for appliqué as it does not fray. Embellish the flower centre with coloured beads.

YOU WILL NEED
• • • • • •

paper and pencil

paper scissors

cotton fabric in two contrasting colours

dressmaker's scissors

assorted felt scraps

fabric glue

dressmaker's pins

sewing machine and matching thread

iron

embroidery thread

crewel needle

coloured beads

PREPARATION

Lay the open book flat on paper and draw round it, adding a 1 cm (½ in) seam allowance. Pin the template to one fabric and cut out. Fold the template in half and cut out two pieces in contrasting fabric, adding an extra 1 cm (½ in) seam allowance to the folded edge. Enlarge the flower motif, draw on to a scrap of felt and cut out. Centre on the right hand side of the first piece of fabric and glue. Cut a flower centre in a different colour felt and glue to the flower.

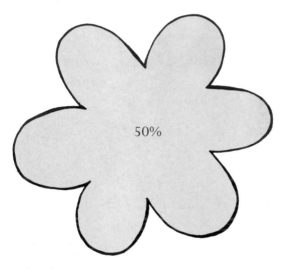

50%

1

Turn under a hem on the long edges of the two contrasting fabric pieces. Stitch and press. Right sides facing, pin to the main piece.

2

Starting at the centre, machine stitch the seams. Clip the corners, press and turn right side out. Position the flower motif on the book cover and stitch round the edge. Stitch the beads to the flower centre.

VALENTINE CARD AND GIFT TAG
· · · · · ·

Make a Valentine card and matching gift tag for a special friend and appliqué them with decorative heart motifs.

YOU WILL NEED
· · · · · ·

coloured card (cardboard)

pencil and ruler

paper scissors

hole punch

assorted fabric scraps

dressmaker's scissors

paper

fabric glue

dressmaker's pins

embroidery thread

crewel needle

small coloured beads

10 cm (4 in) gift cord

PREPARATION

Cut a piece of card (card-board) 15 cm x 20 cm (6 in x 8 in) and fold in half. Cut another piece the same shape as a luggage label and punch a hole in the top. Cut two rectangles from the fabric to suit the size of your card and gift tag. Fray the edges of the fabric using a needle. Cut a strip of fabric with a scalloped edge and glue to the larger rectangular scrap. Enlarge and make a paper template of the heart motif.

50%

1
Pin the heart motifs to contrasting scraps of fabric, and cut out. Cut several small circles in contrasting colours.

2
Glue the circles to the hearts then glue the hearts on to the rectangles. Embellish with beads and colourful stitches. Glue the finished rectangles on to the card and the gift tag. Thread the gift tag with cord and knot.

APPLIQUÉ FELT HAT

This hat is made from felted scraps of knitting. Cool colours which recede, like blues and greens, will look good for the base. In contrast, use hot colours like pink, orange and red for the motifs.

YOU WILL NEED

paper and pencil

paper scissors

dressmaker's scissors

assorted scraps of felted knitting

20 cm x 90 cm (8 in x 36 in) lining fabric

dressmaker's pins

sewing machine and matching thread

petersham

needle and tacking (basting) thread

PREPARATION

Enlarge the paper templates for the hat crown and band and cut out in paper. Cut the pieces out in both felted fabric and lining. Cut out enough felt squares in different colours to fit the band. Draw a design for the crown freehand and cut out in assorted colours of felt.

1
Pin the squares on to the band and zig zag stitch in place. Position your design on the crown and stitch the first layer.

2
Cut more shapes to decorate each square of the band. Appliqué the shapes in layers. Complete the crown design with a second layer of motifs.

3
Machine embroider set stitches in geometric patterns all over both hat pieces.

TO FINISH

Join the short ends of the band to form a tube and stitch to the crown. Make up the lining and place inside the hat, wrong sides facing. Cut the petersham 3 cm (1¼ in) larger than your head measurement plus 1 cm (½ in) seam allowance. Join the short ends and tack (baste) to the lower end of the band. Fold into the hat and top stitch close to the lower edge.

CROWN
25%

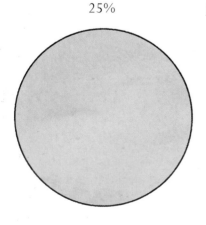

HAT BAND
25%

BLACK-AND-WHITE APPLIQUÉ WAISTCOAT

Appliqué a black design on to plain calico to create this striking waistcoat. Draw the design freehand and stitch small sections at a time.

YOU WILL NEED
......

commercial waistcoat pattern

dressmaker's scissors

90 cm x 150 cm
(36 in x 60 in) calico fabric

50 cm x 90 cm
(20 in x 36 in) black cotton

vanishing marker

dressmaker's pins

sewing machine and
black thread

sharp scissors

PREPARATION

Cut out the waistcoat fronts in both calico and black cotton. Cut the waistcoat back in calico only.

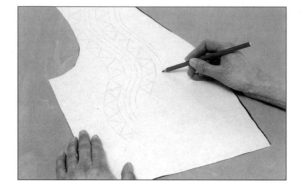

1
Draw a design freehand on to the wrong side of the two calico fronts. Use a vanishing marker.

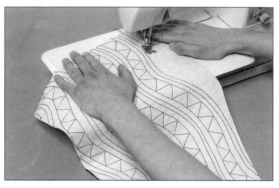

2
Pin the black fronts, right side uppermost, to the right side of the calico fronts. Machine stitch over the drawn lines in black thread.

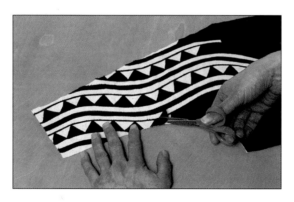

3
Right side facing and following the design, cut away a small section of the top black layer using sharp scissors. Cut close to the stitching line, to expose the calico below.

TO FINISH

Make up the waistcoat, following the pattern instructions.

4
Carefully machine zig zag over all the raw black edges. Cut and machine until the whole piece has been worked.

PINK-AND-NAVY QUILT

This traditionally styled quilt is made up in hot, modern colours. The backing piece is brought over to the front and joins the sashing and borders to make a self-bound edge.

YOU WILL NEED
· · · · · ·

card (cardboard)

craft knife

dressmaker's scissors

50 cm x 90 cm (20 in x 36 in) pink cotton fabric

50 cm x 90 cm (20 in x 36 in) pink-patterned cotton fabric

30 cm x 90 cm (12 in x 36 in) navy-patterned cotton fabric

50 cm x 90 cm (20 in x 36 in) navy cotton fabric

dressmaker's pins

sewing machine and matching thread

iron

1.2 m x 90 cm (48 in x 36 in) wadding (batting)

1.2 m x 90 cm (48 in x 36 in) pink cotton backing fabric

pink and navy quilting thread

crewel needle

PREPARATION

Make card templates 9 cm (3½ in) square. Cut 48 plain pink, 36 pink patterned and 24 navy-patterned fabric squares. Cut four corner templates, 9.5 cm (3¾ in) square, two navy-patterned and two pink. Cut two navy border strips, 9.5 cm x 69 cm (3¾ in x 27¼ in), and two 9.5 cm x 89 cm (3¾ in x 35 in).

1
Arrange the fabric squares and pin together in pairs.

2
Stitch the pairs, using the flag method (see Basic Techniques). Stitch three strips of three squares together to make 12 blocks of nine.

3
Stitch the blocks together, three across and four down. Stitch the corner squares to each end of the short border strips. Press the seams flat. Stitch the long, and then the shorter, borders in place (see Basic Techniques).

4
Trim the wadding (batting) to the same size as the patchwork and sandwich between the patched piece and the backing, right sides out. Pin and tack (baste) through all layers. Bring the backing over to the front, mitre the corners (see Basic Techniques) and slip-stitch to the border. Using the quilting thread, make little navy knots in the centre of each plain pink square and pink knots along the borders.

SIMPLE PATCHWORK CUSHION COVER

Squares of fabric, decorated with buttons, are very effective in these hot, sizzling colours. Finish the corners with pompons. Make the cushion in cotton, satin or velvet.

YOU WILL NEED
......

10 cm x 90 cm (4 in x 36 in) pink fabric

10 cm x 90 cm (4 in x 36 in) orange fabric

10 cm x 90 cm (4 in x 36 in) yellow fabric

dressmaker's scissors

30 cm x 90 cm (12 in x 36 in) backing fabric

dressmaker's pins

sewing machine and matching thread

iron

pink, orange and yellow embroidery thread

crewel needle

9 buttons

4 pompons

PREPARATION

Cut out a total of 16 pink, orange and yellow 9.5 cm (3¾ in) squares. Cut the backing fabric in half to measure 30 cm x 45 cm (12 in x 18 in). Turn under a narrow hem on one short side of each piece.

1
Pin the squares in pairs of different colours. Using the flag method (see Basic Techniques), join in strips of four with a 1 cm (½ in) seam. Press the seams open.

2
Pin and stitch the strips together. Press the seams open.

3
Decorate each square with a row of running stitches round the edge in a contrasting colour. Sew a button to each corner, as shown.

4
Right sides facing, pin the backing fabric to the square patchwork, with one piece slightly overlapping the other. Stitch all the seams. Clip the corners, press and turn right side out. Stitch a pompon to each corner.

SATIN DUFFEL BAG
· · · · · ·

The checker board effect of this patchwork design is enhanced by using strong contrasting colours. The satin is backed with calico, but interfacing could be used instead.

YOU WILL NEED
· · · · · ·

50 cm x 90 cm (20 in x 36 in) calico

dressmaker's scissors

1 m x 90 cm (1 yd x 36 in) black satin fabric

50 cm x 90 cm (20 in x 36 in) yellow satin fabric

needle and tacking (basting) thread

sewing machine and matching thread

50 cm x 90 cm (20 in x 36 in) cotton lining fabric

iron

dressmaker's pins

8 eyelets (grommets)

hammer

1.5 m (1¾ yd) silk cord

PREPARATION

Cut out 36 calico 5 cm (2½ in) squares. Tack (baste) half of the squares to the black satin, and half to the yellow satin. Cut 18 yellow and 18 black squares. Using the flag method (see Basic Techniques), stitch into strips of three, alternating black with yellow. Join the strips into one piece, 12 squares by three. Press the seams. Cut a round base 22 cm (8½ in) in diameter and back with calico cut to the same size. Cut out a rectangle the same size as the patchwork and a base in lining fabric.

1

Cut two strips of black satin 7 cm x 38 cm (2¾ in x 15 in). Press under a 1 cm (½ in) turning, pin and top stitch to either end of the patched piece. Stitch the short ends of the patched piece to form a tube.

2

Pin and stitch the base into the tube. Make up a lining in the same way. Right sides facing, pin the lining to the bag along the top edge. Stitch along the top edge of the bag, leaving a small gap. Clip, press and pull through. Close the gap and top stitch 5 mm (¼ in) from the top.

3

Attach seven equally spaced eyelets (grommets) round the top edge. Fold a satin square into three. Fold the ends in and stitch. Top stitch round the bottom of the bag and attach the remaining eyelets. Thread the cord through the eyelets and tie in a knot.

DIAMOND-IN-A-SQUARE SATIN PURSE

This opulent evening purse is made from a patched piece of richly coloured satin fabric. Follow the diagram at the back of the book for the arrangement of the patches.

YOU WILL NEED

paper and pencil

20 cm x 90 cm (8 in x 36 in) satin fabric, in four colours

dressmaker's scissors

iron-on interfacing

iron

dressmaker's pins

sewing machine and matching thread

20 cm x 30 cm (8 in x 12 in) lining fabric

50 cm (20 in) silk cord

gold bead, with a large hole

PREPARATION

Cut out the patchwork pieces, adding a 5 mm (¼ in) seam allowance. Cut two large 2.5 cm (1 in) squares in colour 1. Enlarge the triangle shape and make a paper template. Cut 16 triangles in both colours 2 and 3. Cut eight 4 cm (1½ in) squares in colour 4. Iron interfacing on to the back of all the patches. Following the diagram for reference, pin and stitch four triangles together then stitch a small square to each end. Make another piece the same. Pin and stitch four more triangles together to make a short strip, and repeat to make a second strip. Stitch either side of one large square. Cut a strip for the casing 32 cm x 7 cm (12½ in x 3 in) in colour 4 and a 11.5 cm (4¼ in) diameter circle for the base in colour 4.

1

Pin and stitch the two narrow patchwork strips either side of the wide one to make a square. Make another patch the same way. Right sides facing, stitch together.

2

Stitch the casing strip to the top edge. Press the seams flat. Fold the piece in half and stitch the side seam. Stitch in the base, trim and clip. Make a lining to fit and insert. Top stitch two rows, 5 mm (¼ in) from the top edge and 5 mm (¼ in) apart, to form a channel. Thread the cord through the channel. Thread on the bead and knot. Fringe the ends of the cord.

PURPLE ZIG ZAG CUSHION

The basic triangle shape can be arranged in different patchwork formations to create various bold geometric patterns.

YOU WILL NEED
• • • • • •

paper and pencil

card (cardboard)

1 m x 90 cm (1 yd x 36 in) dark purple silk fabric

1 m x 90 cm (1 yd x 36 in) pale purple silk fabric

dressmaker's scissors

dressmaker's pins

sewing machine and matching thread

iron

50 cm x 90 cm (20 in x 36 in) backing fabric

PREPARATION

Make card (cardboard) templates of the two triangle shapes. Cut out 21 large and six small triangles in both silk fabrics, adding a 5 mm (¼ in) seam allowance.

1

Arrange the large triangles in six rows to make the zig zag design. To square the ends, place a small half-triangle at the end of each row.

3

Right sides facing, stitch the rows together to make a square. Press the seams.

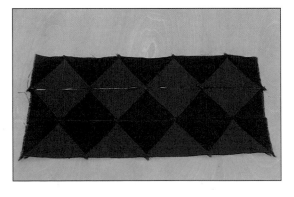

5

Another variation, with the triangles arranged in a diamond pattern.

2

Right sides facing, pin and then stitch the triangles together in contrasting pairs. Press the seams. Stitch the pairs together in rows. Press.

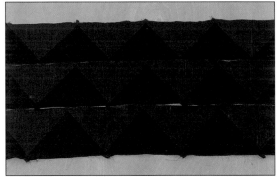

4

This alternative shows the triangles arranged in a mountain design.

TO FINISH

Right sides facing, join the patchwork pieces to the backing fabric to make an envelope cushion cover (see Basic Techniques).

50%

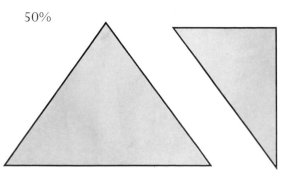

HEART NEEDLECASE

Appliqué a padded heart on to a silk needlecase and embellish it with metallic thread and tiny bugle beads. The needlecase is constructed like a book, with felt pages stitched inside.

YOU WILL NEED

paper and pencil

card (cardboard)

paper scissors

6 cm (2½ in) square turquoise silk fabric

19 cm x 12 cm (7½ in x 4¾ in) purple silk fabric

embroidery scissors

needle and tacking (basting) thread

dressmaker's pins

needle and matching thread

scrap of wadding (batting)

metallic thread

embroidery needle

small gold bugle beads

fabric glue

scraps of felt

28 cm (11 in) fine turquoise ribbon

PREPARATION

Trace the heart motif and make a paper template. Cut out two pieces of card (cardboard) 9 cm x 7 cm (3½ in x 2¾ in).

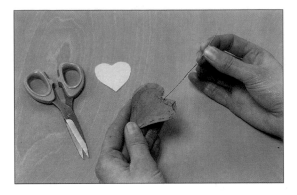

1

Draw round the template on to the turquoise silk and cut out, adding a 5 mm (¼ in) seam allowance. Clip the seam allowance, turn under and tack (baste).

2

Centre the heart on the righthand side of the purple silk rectangle, and appliqué. From the wrong side, slit the fabric behind the heart and fill with wadding (batting). Close the slit. Embellish the heart with metallic thread and bugle beads and the silk with cross stitches.

3

Glue the two pieces of card on to the reverse of the purple silk. Fold over the silk, mitre the corners and stick down. Lay a piece of felt, cut to size, over the pieces of card and slip-stitch (see Basic Techniques) to the silk.

4

Layer felt rectangles for the book paper inside the case. Stitch them together along the fold line. Thread the ribbon through the book from back to front, and tie in a bow.

SNAKES AND LADDERS

· · · · · · ·

This patchwork playmat doubles as a snakes and ladders board. It is constructed like a quilt, so you could make it large enough to cover a child's bed.

YOU WILL NEED
· · · · · ·

card (cardboard) and pencil

30 cm x 90 cm (12 in x 36 in) cotton fabric

dressmaker's scissors

scraps of coloured felt

vanishing marker

craft knife

sewing machine and matching thread

black embroidery thread

crewel needle

50 cm x 90 cm (20 in x 36 in) backing fabric

dressmaker's pins

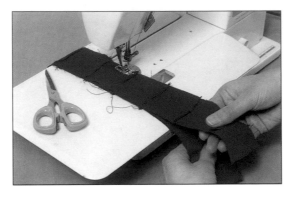

1
Stitch the squares together in strips of ten. Stitch all ten strips together to make a square.

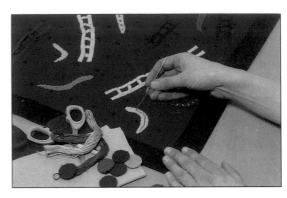

2
Number the squares, using black embroidery stitches. Appliqué the snakes and ladders on to the mat.

PREPARATION

Make a 3 cm (1¼ in) square card (cardboard) template. Cut out 100 squares from the cotton fabric, adding a 5 mm (¼ in) seam allowance. Draw snakes, ladders and counters freehand on to the felt scraps and cut out.

TO FINISH

Cut the backing 3 cm (1¼ in) bigger than the mat all round. Wrong sides facing, pin to the mat. Bring the backing over to the front, mitre the corners and stitch the borders (see Basic Techniques).

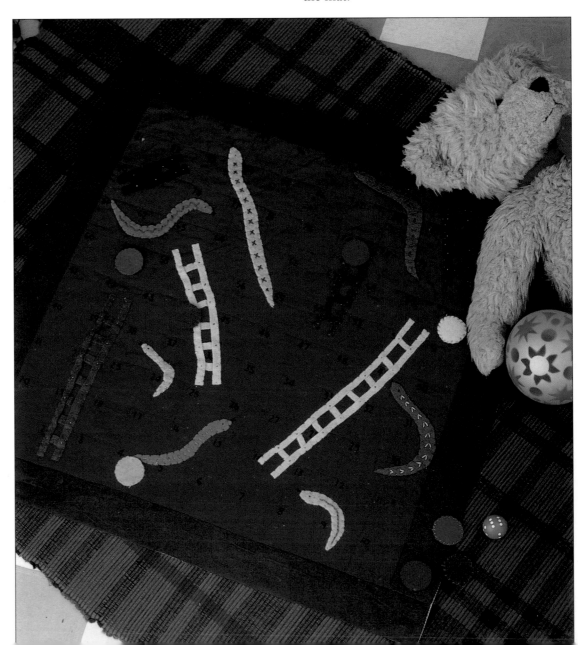

CHILD'S BLANKET

Small children will love to snuggle up under this cosy blanket. It is appliquéd by hand with colourful circles decorated with buttons.

YOU WILL NEED
. . . . . .

blanket fabric

dressmaker's scissors

tapestry wool

crewel needle

saucer

fabric marker

assorted scraps of coloured woollen or blanket fabric

large buttons

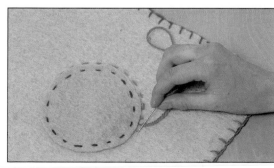

1
Cut the blanket to the size required, turn under a small hem and blanket stitch the edge in different colours (see Basic Techniques).

2
Draw round a saucer on to the scraps of fabric and cut out circles. Hand appliqué to the blanket in running stitch. Sew a button to the centre of each circle.

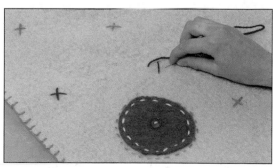

3
Work large cross stitches in a contrasting colour to fill the background fabric.

SHOE BAG

Choose an appropriate shoe to appliqué to this witty drawstring bag. A ballet shoe or gym shoe would also look good.

YOU WILL NEED

dressmaker's scissors

50 cm x 90 cm (20 in x 36 in) cotton fabric

sewing machine and matching thread

65 cm x 7 cm (26 in x 2¾ in) contrasting fabric

iron

paper and pencil

fabric marker

assorted fabric scraps

iron-on fusible bonding web

dressmaker's pins

scrap of narrow ribbon

50 cm (20 in) of 2.5 cm (1 in) wide ribbon

small button

PREPARATION

Cut the fabric to make a rectangle 45 cm x 70 cm (17¾ in x 27½ in). Fold 6.5 cm (2½ in) to the right side on one long edge, and machine stitch. Right sides facing, fold the rectangle in half and stitch round the base and sides of the bag. Turn right side out. Cut a contrasting strip 66 cm x 7 cm (26 in x 2¾ in) and press under a 5 mm (¼ in) hem on the long sides. Enlarge the template of the shoe motif, and trace on to the fabric scraps. Iron on to the bonding web and cut out.

1

Starting at the seam, pin the contrasting strip to the right side of the bag, 5 cm (2 in) from the top. Top stitch the long edges by hand, leaving the short ends open.

2

Peel the backing off the bonding web and iron the shoe to the bag. Decorate the shoe with hand stitches and a small ribbon bow.

3

Thread the contrasting fabric channel with the wide ribbon. Fold under the raw ends of the ribbon, then join together by stitching the button through both ends.

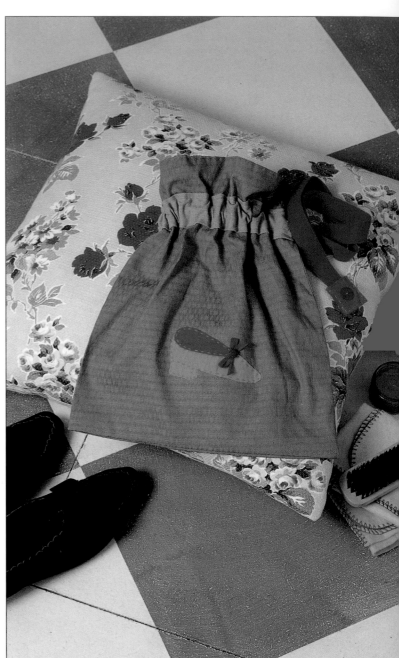

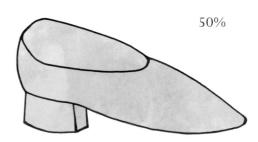

50%

PATCHWORK TOY BAG

Stitch a piece of rainbow patchwork to make into a large toy bag. The colours run in diagonal lines to look like steps.

YOU WILL NEED

paper and pencil

card (cardboard)

craft knife

scraps of fabric, in six rainbow colours

iron-on interfacing

iron

sewing machine and matching thread

30 cm (12 in) wooden coat hanger

vanishing marker

red paint, optional

1

Right sides facing, stitch the two small blocks together along half their length. Press the seam allowance along the opening. Tack (baste) and then top-stitch to neaten the right side.

2

Right sides facing, pin the two bag pieces together. Lay the coat hanger on the top edge and draw round it. Cut along the curved line.

PREPARATION

Make a 10 cm (4 in) square template in card (cardboard) and cut 72 patches from the interfacing. Iron the interfacing to the fabric scraps and cut out, adding a 5 mm (¼ in) seam allowance. Arrange them in diagonal lines to form rainbow steps. Using the flag method (see Basic Techniques), join half of the squares into two blocks, each six by three. Press the seams flat. Make a large block, six squares by six, for the back of the bag.

TO FINISH

Stitch the two pieces together with a 1 cm (½ in) seam allowance. Clip the corners, press and turn through. Paint the coat hanger, if wished, and fit into the bag.

MOSAIC CUSHION
· · · · · ·

This patchwork technique mimics that of mosaic. Small pieces of fabric are sewn together by hand
to create an all-over design.

YOU WILL NEED

paper and pencil

craft knife

dressmaker's pins

*50 cm x 90 cm
(20 in x 36 in)
red cotton fabric*

*scraps of black, grey and
white cotton fabric*

dressmaker's scissors

*needle and tacking
(basting) thread*

matching thread

embroidery scissors

*sewing machine and
matching thread*

polyester wadding (batting)

1
Enlarge the design and make
paper templates of all the
shapes. Decide on a colour
scheme and mark each shape.

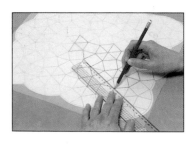

2
Pin the paper templates to the
back of the scraps of fabric
and cut out, adding a 5 mm
(¼ in) seam allowance.

3
Tack (baste) the fabric shapes
to the paper templates.

4
Oversew the patches together,
using neat whip stitches (see
Basic Techniques). Follow the
diagram for reference. Work
on a small section at a time.

50%

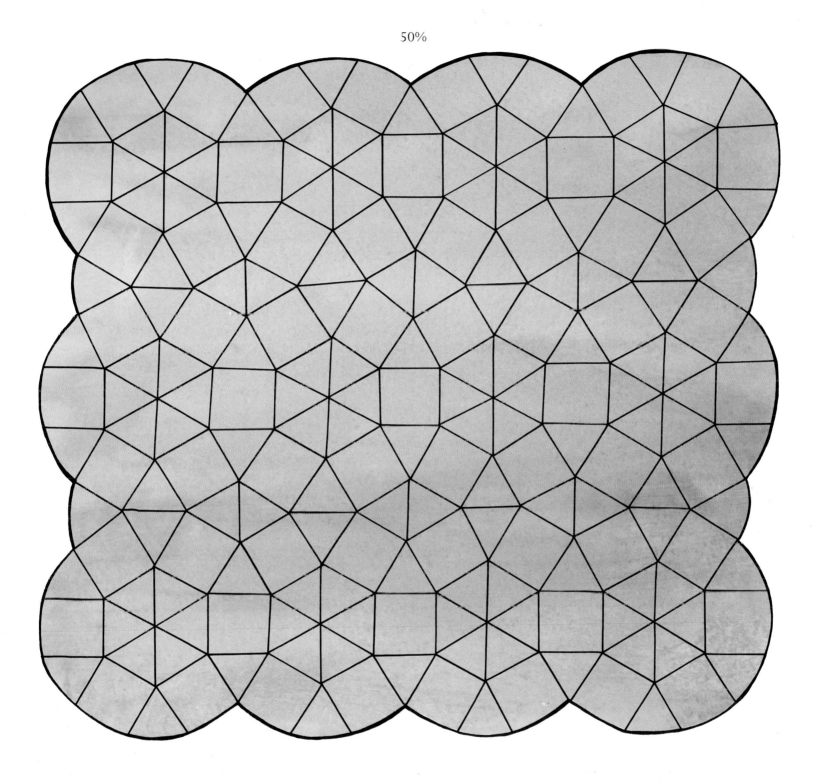

TO FINISH

Remove the tacking (basting) threads and paper templates, and press the seams flat. Cut the red cotton backing fabric to fit the patched piece and place together, right sides facing. Machine stitch round the edges, leaving a gap. Trim and clip the corners, turn right side out and fill with wadding (batting). Slip-stitch the gap closed.

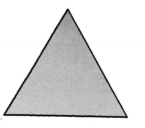

KITCHEN APRON

Make a bright apron with an unusual scalloped border and appliqué kitchen utensils on to it with colourful hand stitches.

YOU WILL NEED

paper and pencil
card (cardboard)
craft knife
fabric scraps
iron-on interfacing
iron
75 cm x 90 cm
(30 in x 36 in) cotton fabric
dressmaker's scissors
75 cm x 90 cm
(30 in x 36 in)
contrasting cotton fabric
vanishing marker
embroidery thread
crewel needle
dressmaker's pins
sewing machine and
matching thread
iron
1 m (1 yd) of 8 cm (3 in)
wide ribbon

PREPARATION

Enlarge the knife, fork and spoon motifs and cut out in card (cardboard). Cut a semi-circle in thin card. Iron the interfacing to the reverse of the fabric scraps. Cut a front in cotton fabric, 60 cm x 50 cm (24 in x 20 in). Cut a backing piece in the contrasting fabric to match.

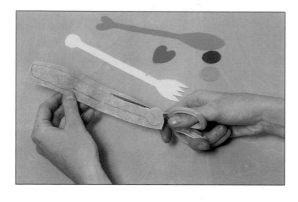

1

Draw round the templates on to the interfacing. Cut out in different colours.

3

Right sides facing, match the front to the backing and pin. Draw round the semi-circle along the reverse of the lower edge, to mark a scalloped line. Machine stitch round three sides, leaving the top open. Clip the corners and the scalloped edge.

5

Fold under the open edge and press. Press the ribbon in half lengthways. Tack (baste) and top stitch round the top edge.

2

Appliqué the motifs to the apron front with large, colourful hand stitches.

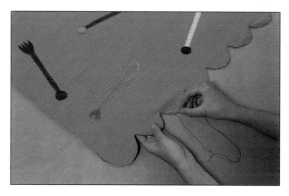

4

Turn the apron right side out. Stitch a line of running stitches along the scalloped edge.

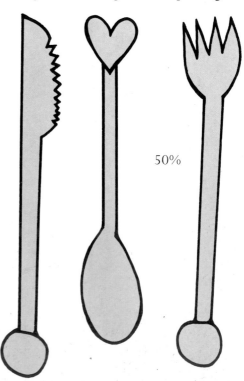

50%

APPLIQUÉ PILLOWSLIP

Appliqué these brightly coloured stars and hearts on to a ready-made pillowslip and decorate with simple stitches. This is an easy way to brighten up faded bedlinen.

YOU WILL NEED

paper and pencil

paper scissors

fabric marker

iron-on fusible bonding web

iron

assorted fabric scraps

dressmaker's scissors

pillowslip

assorted embroidery threads

crewel needle

1

Make paper templates of the heart and star motifs. Trace on to the bonding web. Iron the bonding web on to the reverse of the fabric scraps and cut out the motifs.

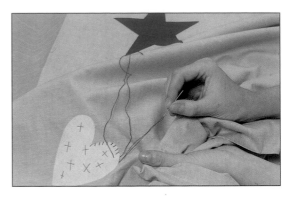

2

Peel off the backing paper and iron a motif to each corner of the pillowslip. Blanket stitch round the edge (see Basic Techniques) and decorate with embroidery stitches.

3

Sew a running stitch in a contrasting thread on both sides of the pillowcase.

50%

50%

WASH BAG

· · · · · ·

This little bathroom bag is made from washable fabric. It has a very unusual, asymmetrical patchwork design reminiscent of Art Deco.

YOU WILL NEED

paper and pencil

card (cardboard)

craft knife

dressmaker's scissors

30 cm x 90 cm (12 in x 36 in) white PVC

30 cm x 90 cm (12 in x 36 in) red PVC

30 cm x 90 cm (12 in x 36 in) blue PVC

dressmaker's pins

sewing machine and matching thread

71 cm (28 in) thick white cotton cord

PREPARATION

Enlarge the shapes and cut out in card (cardboard). Following the numbers on the plan, cut out the patches in PVC, adding a 5 mm (¼ in) seam allowance, as follows: cut numbers 1, 6, 13, 14 and 15 in white; 2, 3, 8, 10 and 12 in red; 4, 5, 7, 9 and 11 in blue. Cut a 38 cm x 30 cm (15 in x 12 in) lining in white PVC. Cut a blue PVC 18 cm (7 in) square for the back of the bag.

TO FINISH

Right sides facing, stitch the patch to the blue back piece along one long seam. Stitch the lining to the top of the bag. Clip and trim the seam. Fold in half lengthways and stitch round the seams, leaving a small gap. Pull through then fold in the lining, leaving a 6 cm (2½ in) band at the top. Stitch two parallel lines 5 mm (¼ in) from the top edge, 1 cm (½ in) apart, for the channel. Thread the cord through the channel and knot the ends.

1

The patch is made in two halves. To stitch the first half, join blue 4 to red 2. Join blue 5 to red 3. Next, join 4/2 to white 6. Join 3/5 to white 6. Join the whole piece to white 1.

2

To stitch the second half, join blue 9 to red 10. Join 9/10 to white 14. Join red 10 to blue 11. Join 10/11 to white 13. Join blue 11 to red 12. Join blue 9 to red 8. Join 8/9 to white 15. Join blue 7 to red 8. Stitch the patches together.

50%

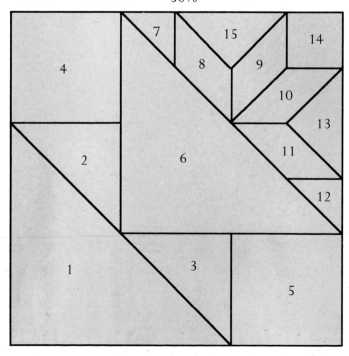

HOT WATER BOTTLE COVER

· · · · · ·

Strip patchwork is used for this jazzy cover, which is then quilted with a scroll and diamond pattern. The layers of padding will help to keep your hot water bottle warm on cold winter nights.

YOU WILL NEED

1 m x 90 cm
(1 yd x 36 in) white fabric

dressmaker's scissors

50 cm x 90 cm
(20 in x 36 in) black fabric

sewing machine and
matching thread

hot water bottle

vanishing marker

50 cm x 90 cm
(20 in x 36 in)
wadding (batting)

red thread

2 m (2 yd) of 2.5 cm (1 in)
black bias binding

dressmaker's pins

iron

3 press studs (snap fasteners)

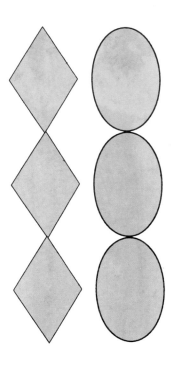

QUILTING DESIGNS 50%

PREPARATION

Cut the white fabric into four and the black into six 50 cm x 7.5 cm (19¾ in x 3 in) strips. Join the strips together lengthways in two sets of five, alternating the colours. Trace round a hot water bottle on to the patched pieces, add a 1 cm (½ in) seam allowance and cut out. Cut out two pieces the same from the white fabric for the lining. Trace and draw the quilting design on to the cover pieces.

1

Sandwich the wadding (batting) between the patched pieces and the lining, right sides facing out. Tack (baste) through all the layers. Stitch round the edge on both pieces. Stitch the quilting design in red.

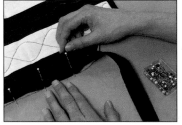

2

Bind the top edge with the bias binding. Pin another strip of bias binding round the side edges on the right side and stitch to the cover. Bind the second side. Place the two sides together, right sides facing, with the binding sandwiched between. Stitch round the seam line, leaving a 15 cm (6 in) opening at the top. Trim and press.

3

Turn right side out and slip-stitch the opening. Attach the press studs (snap fasteners) to the top edge of the cover.

HEART BROOCH

This tiny appliqué heart made from scraps of fabric is embellished with gold thread. Mounted on a brooch back it makes a pretty badge, but it could also be appliquéd directly on to a pocket or the corner of a shirt collar.

YOU WILL NEED

paper and pencil
scrap of gold velvet or silk
sharp embroidery scissors
scraps of blue and grey woollen fabric
iron-on interfacing
iron
sewing machine and gold thread
scrap of cream organza
dressmaker's pins
brooch back

PREPARATION

Draw the heart shape, transfer it to the gold velvet or silk scrap and cut out. Cut a scrap of blue fabric 3 cm x 4 cm (1¼ in x 1½ in), and a scrap of grey fabric, 5 cm x 4 cm (2 in x 1½ in). Iron the grey fabric to the interfacing. Machine several lines of the gold thread in a square to make a frame.

1

Place the blue fabric on to the frame, then the heart, and finally cover with a scrap of organza and pin. Machine stitch the organza to the backing close to the gold frame. Trim the organza back to the stitch line.

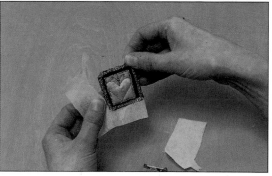

2

Pull the interfacing away from round the brooch. Sew the brooch back to the underside.

CHILD'S APRON

This painting apron is constructed from strips of fabric. It has a roomy pocket for pens and paintbrushes, trimmed with pompon tape. This apron is made in cotton, but you could also use stain-resistant PVC fabric.

YOU WILL NEED

dressmaker's scissors

scraps of fabric

paper and pencil

50 cm x 90 cm
(20 in x 36 in) cotton fabric

sewing machine and
matching thread

iron

25 cm (10 in) pompon tape

dressmaker's pins

needle and tacking
(basting) thread

1.5 m (60 in) of 8 cm (3 in)
wide ribbon

PREPARATION

Cut five 6 cm x 20 cm (2½ in x 8 in) strips of assorted fabric for the pocket. Draw the apron shape on paper, and cut out in cotton fabric. Machine stitch under a hem all round the apron.

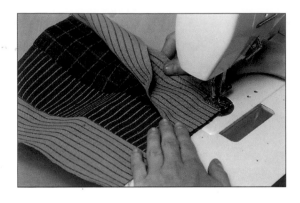

1

Stitch the strips together to make one piece. Cut a piece of cotton fabric to the same size. Right sides facing, pin and stitch the seams, leaving a small gap. Clip the corners, press and turn through.

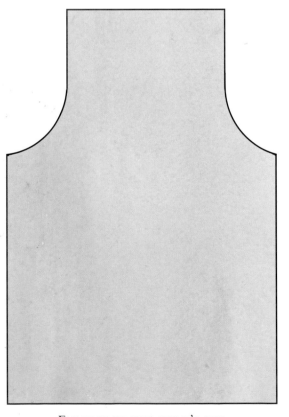

ENLARGE TO THE CHILD'S SIZE

2

Slip-stitch the pompon tape to the top edge of the patched piece.

3

Tack (baste) the pocket to the apron and top stitch.

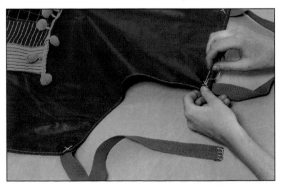

4

Press the ribbon in half lengthways. Cut a 61 cm (24 in) length and sew to either side of the top edge. Cut the rest of ribbon in half and sew either side of the waist. Neaten the ends.

PVC BAG
· · · · · ·

This bag shows how unusual fabrics can create an effect completely different to traditional patchwork.
Clip the curved seams to ensure a smooth fit.

YOU WILL NEED

paper and pencil

card (cardboard)

craft knife

dressmaker's scissors

1 m (1 yd) wadding (batting)

1 m x 90 cm
(1 yd x 36 in) blue PVC

50 cm x 90 cm
(20 in x 36 in) red PVC

50 cm x 90 cm
(20 in x 36 in) white PVC

dressmaker's pins

sewing machine and
matching thread

iron

needle and tacking
(basting) thread

knitting needle

TO FINISH

Stitch the side edges of the patched pieces to make a tube. Pin and stitch in the base. Trim and clip the seams. Pin the handles to the bag. Stitch the blue PVC lining to the top of the bag, securing the handles at the same time and leaving a 7.5 cm (3 in) gap. Pull the lining through and slip-stitch the gap. Press the bag under paper.

PREPARATION

Enlarge the design from the back of the book and cut out two complete bag pieces in blue PVC for the lining and a wadding (batting) piece, adding a 1 cm (½ in) seam allowance. Cut out two of each patch shape in red and white PVC, adding 5 mm (¼ in) seam allowance. Cut a red and blue PVC base and a wadding base, adding a 1 cm (½ in) seam allowance. Cut two red handles 36 cm x 10 cm (14 in x 4 in).

1

Join patches, 1 and 3 to 2. Join 4 and 6 to 5. Join 7 and 9 to 8, and 10 and 12 to 11. Clip, and press the seams carefully under a piece of paper, using a cool iron. Join together to make two large squares, then join the squares together. Make two pieces the same. Clip and press the seams flat.

2

Place the two patched pieces and the red base on to the wadding (batting), and tack (baste) round the edges.

3

Make up the blue PVC lining.

4

Stitch the red handle strips lengthways. Turn through and fill with wadding (batting), using a knitting needle. Pull through the wadding and trim off 2½ cm (1 in) at the ends.

TEMPLATES

HISTORIC STYLE

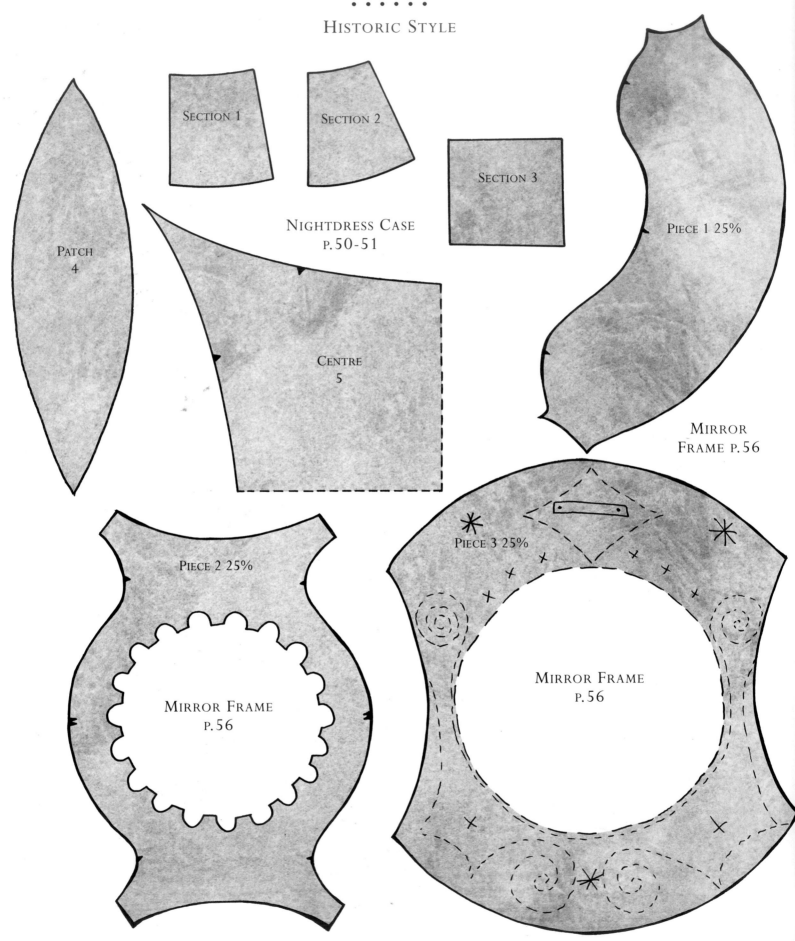

PATCH
4

SECTION 1

SECTION 2

SECTION 3

NIGHTDRESS CASE
P. 50-51

CENTRE
5

PIECE 1 25%

MIRROR
FRAME P. 56

PIECE 2 25%

MIRROR FRAME
P. 56

PIECE 3 25%

MIRROR FRAME
P. 56

QUILTED CURTAIN P. 58
MOTIFS 50%

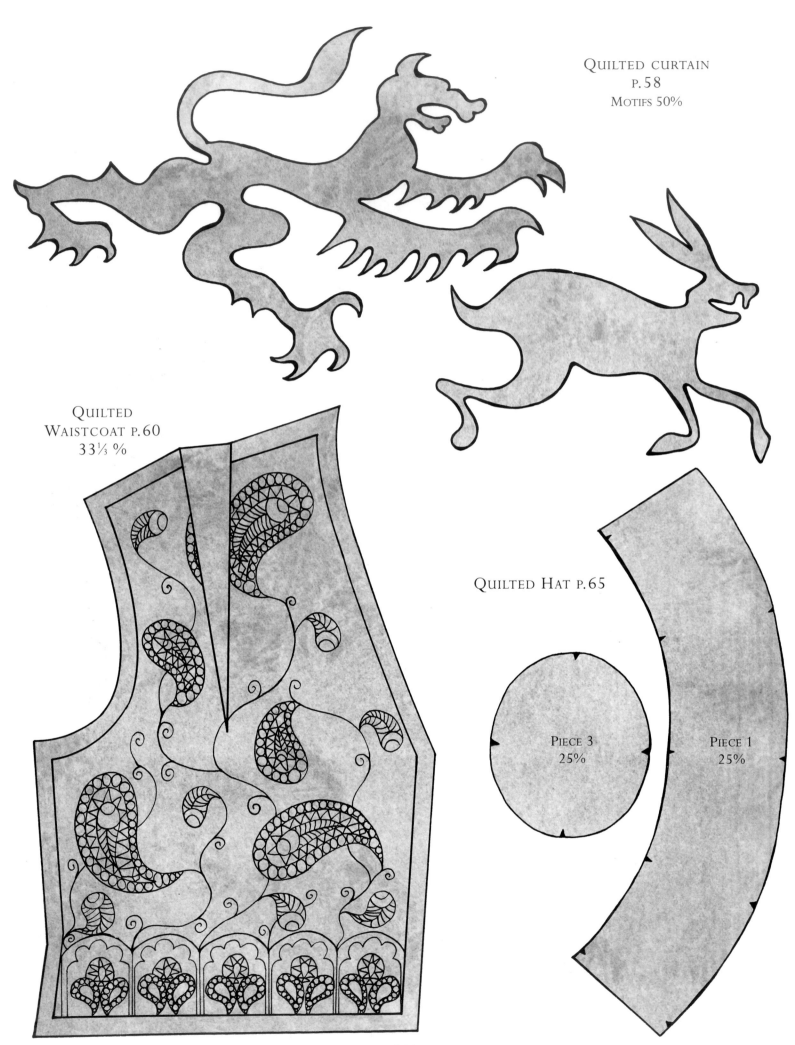

QUILTED CURTAIN
P. 58
MOTIFS 50%

QUILTED
WAISTCOAT P. 60
33⅓ %

QUILTED HAT P. 65

PIECE 3
25%

PIECE 1
25%

QUILTED HAT
P.65

PIECE 2
25%

BAG 50%

HANDLE 50%

SIDE PIECE
50%

SATIN HANDBAG
P.76

BRODERIE PERSE
APPLIQUÉ
NAPKINS P.71

COUNTRY STYLE

COUNTRY THROW P.84
MOTIFS 50%

HEART

GRAPES

HAND

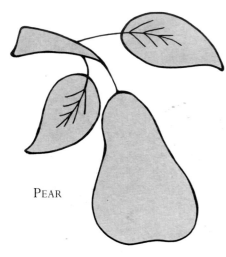

PEAR

BIRD 2

BIRD 1

FLOWER

STRAWBERRY

BIRD 3

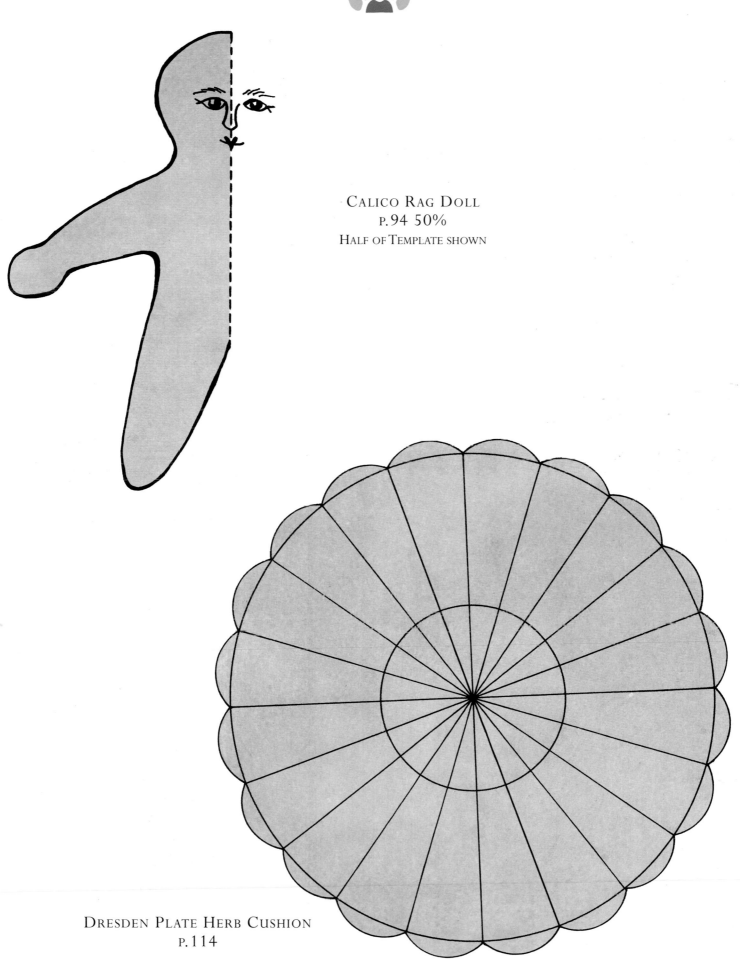

CALICO RAG DOLL
P. 94 50%
HALF OF TEMPLATE SHOWN

DRESDEN PLATE HERB CUSHION
P. 114

SOLE 50%

TOP 50%

CHERRY BASKET PATCHWORK QUILT
P.120 50%

CRAZY PATCHWORK
BOOTEES P.122

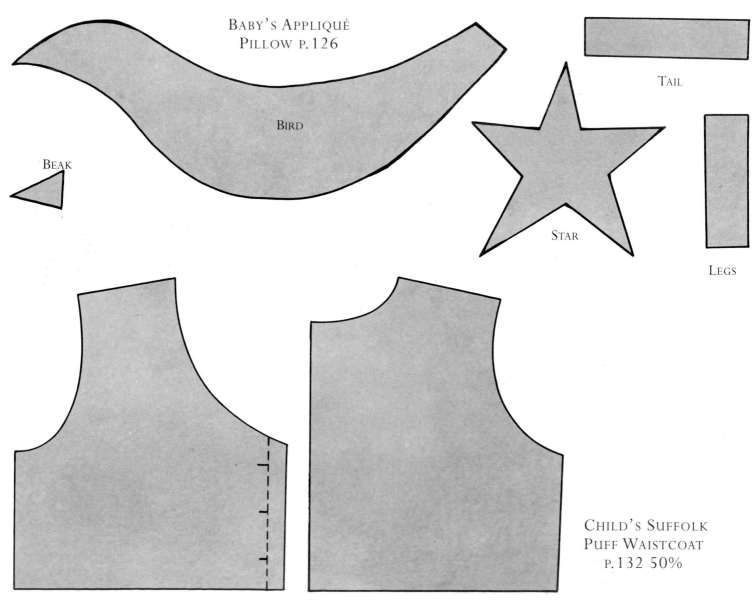

BABY'S APPLIQUÉ
PILLOW P.126

BIRD

BEAK

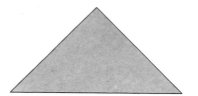

TAIL

STAR

LEGS

CHILD'S SUFFOLK
PUFF WAISTCOAT
P.132 50%

TEMPLATES

ETHNIC STYLE

PATCHWORK
DUFFLE BAG
P. 138 50%

SAN BLAS OVEN
MITTS P. 143

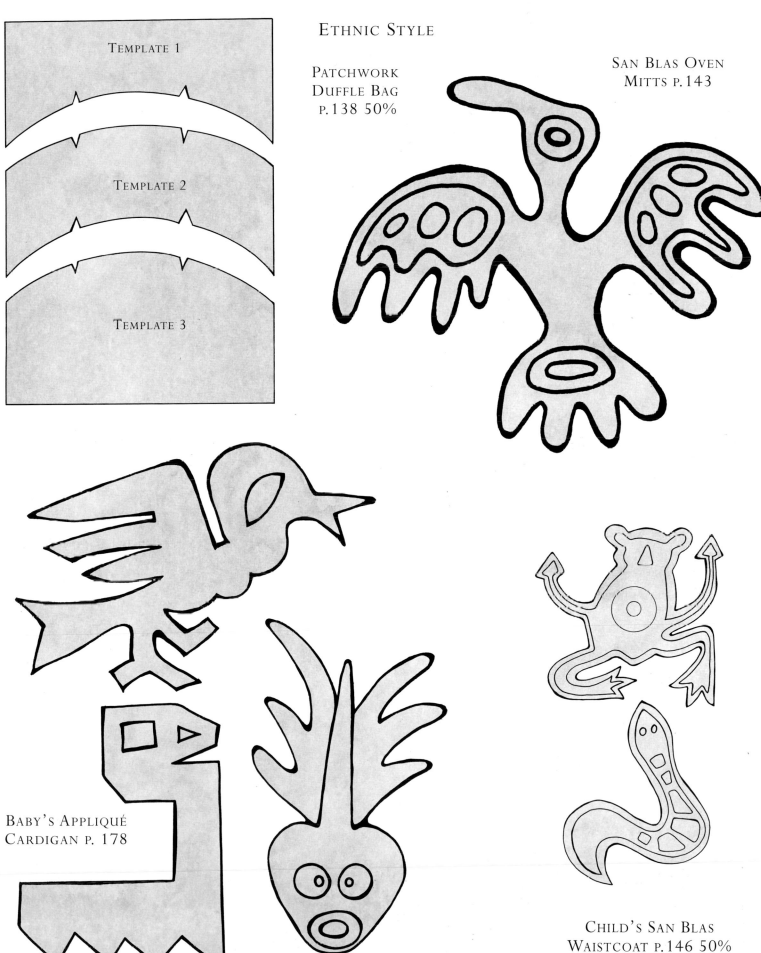

TEMPLATE 1

TEMPLATE 2

TEMPLATE 3

BABY'S APPLIQUÉ
CARDIGAN P. 178

CHILD'S SAN BLAS
WAISTCOAT P. 146 50%

PA NDUA
APPLIQUÉ FRAME
P. 170

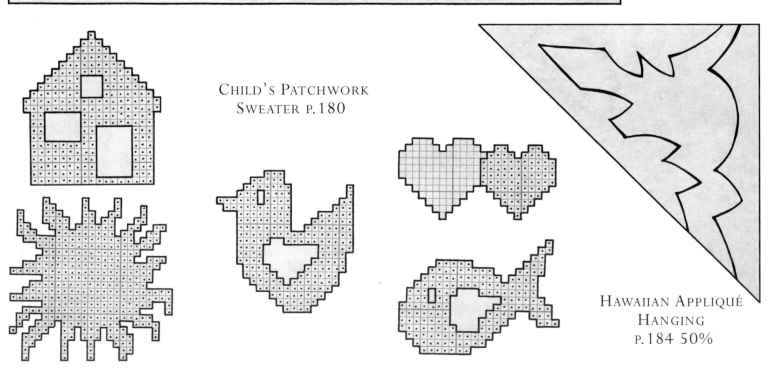

CHILD'S PATCHWORK
SWEATER P. 180

HAWAIIAN APPLIQUÉ
HANGING
P. 184 50%

CONTEMPORARY STYLE

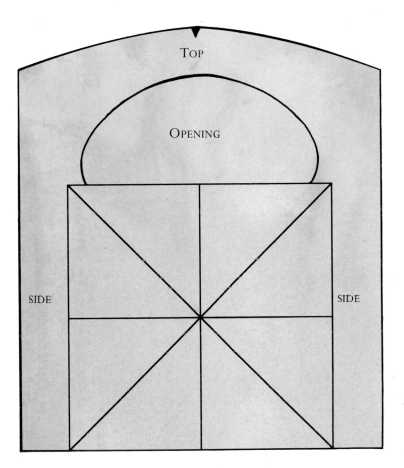

PEG BAG P.192
50%

Top

Opening

SIDE   SIDE

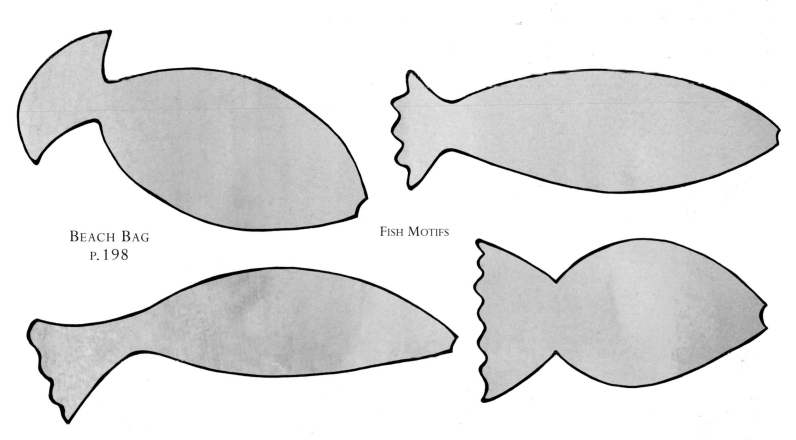

BEACH BAG
P.198

FISH MOTIFS

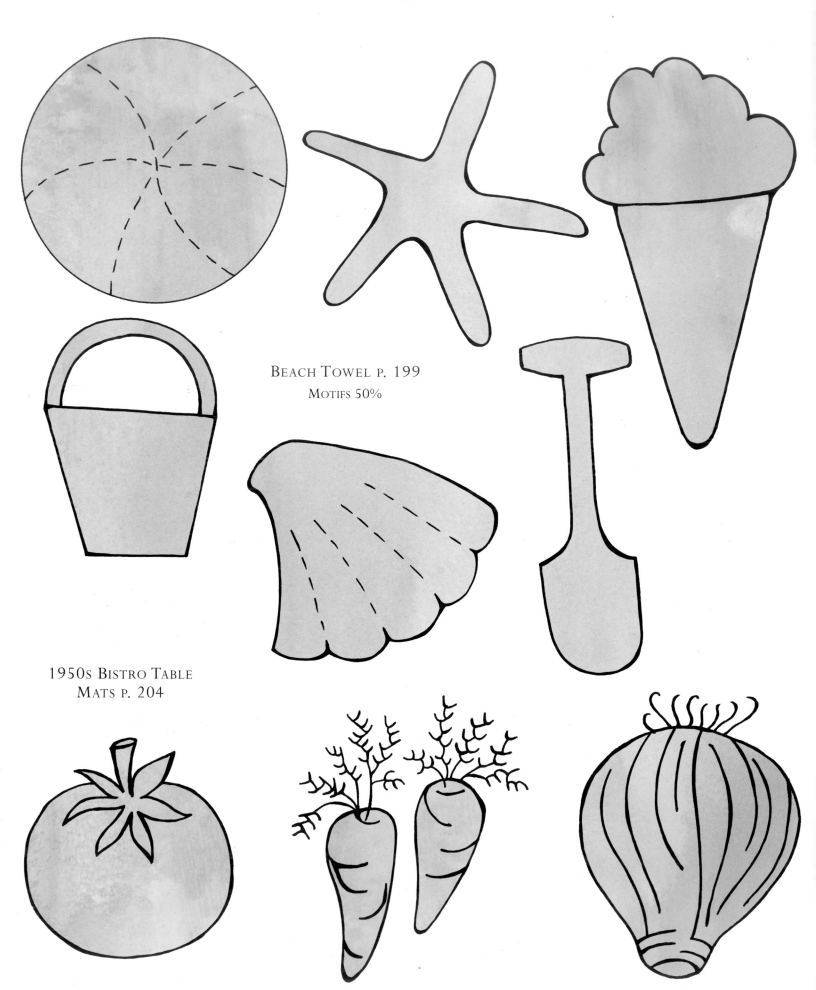

BEACH TOWEL P. 199
MOTIFS 50%

1950S BISTRO TABLE
MATS P. 204

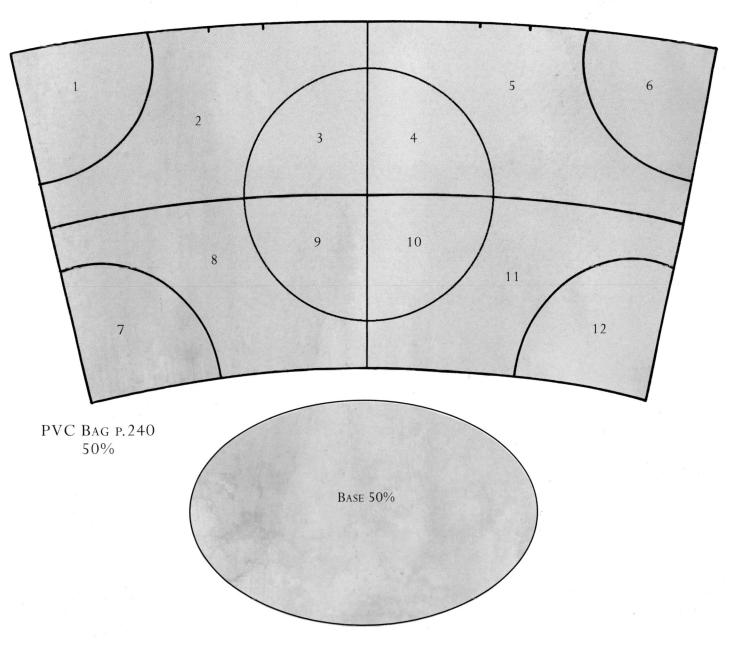

DIAMOND-IN-A-
SQUARE SATIN
PURSE P.221 50%

PVC BAG P.240
50%

BASE 50%

INDEX
· · · · · ·

A
acetate templates, 19
acid-free paper, 10
adhesives, 8
Amish Bag, 86
appliqué
  fabrics, 22
  techniques, 22
Appliqué Book Cover, 212
Appliqué Felt Ball, 164
Appliqué Felt Hat, 214
Appliqué Glasses Case, 206
Appliqué Pillowslip, 234
Appliqué Sunflower, 181
Appliqué T Shirt, 98
Appliqué Wool Scarf, 89
aprons, 232, 238
Autumn Leaf Shoe Bag, 99

B
Baby Blanket, 166
Baby's Appliqué Cardigan, 178
  template, 249
Baby's Appliqué Pillow, 126
  templates, 248
backing papers, attaching, 19
bags, 25, 48, 70, 86, 99, 104,
  106, 138, 139, 145, 156,
  163, 192, 194, 198, 220,
  228, 229, 235
  templates, 240, 249, 251,
  253
balls, 164
basting
  appliqué, 22
  quilts, 21
  thread, 10
Bathroom Curtains, 37
batting, 10
  quilts, 21
Beach Bag, 198
  template, 251
Beach Towel, 199
  template, 252
Beaded Purse, 187
beads, 10
bears, 44
beeswax, 8
berets, 196
between needles, 8
bias binding, 10
  mitred corners, 25
bias strips
  making, 25
  using, 25

Black-and-white Appliqué
  Cover, 200
Black-and-white Appliqué
  Waistcoat, 216
blanket stitch, 23
blankets, 166, 227
Bolster Cushion, 92, 160
bonding web, 10, 22
Book Cover, 162
book covers, 150, 162, 212
books, 96
bootees, 122
  template, 248
borders, patchwork, 20
box patchwork, 20
Boxes, 172
  quilted, 63
Broderie Perse Appliqué
  Napkins, 71
  templates, 247
Broderie Perse Appliqué
  Tablecloth, 72
brooches, 237
buttons, 10

C
calico, 12
Calico Bag, 139
Calico Napkin, 174
Calico Rag Doll, 94
  template, 247
Cameo Picture, 55
carbon paper, 10, 24
card templates, 18
cardigans, 178
  template, 249
cards, 116, 148, 204, 213
Cathedral Window Needle
  Case, 40
chalk, 8
Cherry Basket Patchwork

Cushion, 120
  templates, 248
Child's Apron, 238
Child's Berry, 196
Child's Blanket, 227
Child's Patchwork Sweater, 180
  template, 250
Child's San Blas Waistcoat, 146
  template, 249
Child's Skirt, 74
Child's Strip Patchwork
  Rucksack, 104
Child's Strip Patchwork Skirt,
  105
Child's Strip Patchwork
  Waistcoat, 108
Child's Suffolk Puff Waistcoat,
  132
  templates, 248
choosing fabrics, 14–16
Christmas cards, 204
coat hangers, 151
colour, fabrics, 15–16
contemporary style, 189–241
  templates, 251–3
Corded Purse, 52
Corded Quilt, 53
corduroy, 12
corners, mitred, 20
cotton
  fabric, 12, 14
  thread, 10
country style, 80–131
  templates, 246–8
Country Throw, 84
  templates, 246
Country Wreath Cushion, 93
craft knife, 8
Crazy Patchwork Bootees, 122
  template, 248
Crazy Patchwork Cushion, 32
Crazy Patchwork Pram Quilt,
  140
crewel needles, 8
Crib Quilt, 66, 141
cubes, 126
Curtain Tie-backs, 158
curtains, 37, 157
  tie-backs, 158
curved templates, 19
cushions, 32, 69, 92, 93, 114,
  120, 128, 144, 160, 186, 202,
  222, 230
  covers, 25, 219
  templates, 247, 248
cutting tools, 8

D
designs
  enlarging, 24
  transferring, 24
Diamond and Square Quilt,
  118
Diamond-in-a-square Satin
  Purse, 221
  template, 253
dolls, 94
  template, 247
drawstring bags, 25, 145
Dresden Plate Herb Cushion,
  114
  template, 247
dress velvet, 12
dresses, 74
dressmaker's carbon paper, 10
dressmaker's paper, 10
dressmaker's scissors, 8
dressmaker's wheel, 8
duffle bags, 138, 220
  templates, 249
dyes, 8

E
egg cosies, 112, 169
embroidery frames, 8
embroidery hoops, 8
embroidery scissors, 8
embroidery threads, 10
enlarging a design, 24
envelope cushion cover, 25
equipment, 8
ethnic style, 135–87
  templates, 249–50
eyelets, 10

F
fabrics, 12
  appliqué, 22
  choosing, 14–16
  colour, 15–16
  dyes, 8
  finding the grain, 24
  glue, 8
  patterned, 16
  textured, 16
  tone, 15
felt, 12
fine-wale corduroy, 12
flag method, 20
Folded-star Pin Cushion, 42
frames, 8, 170, 250
  mirror, 56, 242
  patchwork, 88

photo, 117
  satin patchwork, 68
fusible bonding web, 10, 22

G
gauges, 8
Gift Tags, 152, 213
gingham, 12
glasses cases, 206
glues, 8
Gothic Jewels, 78
grain, fabric, 24
graph paper, 10
Greetings Card, 148
grommets, 10

H
hand piercing, 20
hand quilting, 21
handbags, 76, 245
Hanging Fan, 131
Hanging Heart Sachet, 102
Hanging Hearts, 130
hangings, 184, 208
  template, 250
Hatpin Cushion, 34
hats, 64, 176, 196, 214
  templates, 244–5
Hawaiian Appliqué Hanging,
  184
  templates, 250
Heart Appliqué Pillowslip, 103
Heart Brooch, 237
Heart Needlecase, 224
herb cushions, 114
  templates, 247
Hexagon Pin Cushion, 121
historic style, 27–79
  templates, 242–5
history, 7
Holbein stitch, 23
hoops, 8
Hot Water Bottle Cover, 236

I
interfacing, 10
  backing with, 19
iron-on fusible bonding web,
  10, 22
iron-on interfacing, 10
irons, 8
isometric paper, 10

J
Jam Jar Cover, 205
Jewellery Roll, 207

jewels, 78
joining patches, 20

K
Kantha Quilt, 182
key rings, 100
Kitchen Apron, 232
knifes, craft, 8

L
lace, 10
Lavender Bag, 48
lavender sachets, 48, 102
lawn, 12
LeMoyne Star, 48
linen, 12
Little House Key Ring, 100
log cabin patchwork, 20
Log Cabin Throw, 110

M
machine embroidery thread, 10
machine piercing, 20
machine quilting, 21
markers, 8
materials, 10
measuring tools, 8
Medieval Quilt, 58
  template, 243
Mirror Frame, 56
  template, 242
mitred corners
  binding, 25
  patchwork, 20
Mosaic Cushion, 230
mounting pictures, 25
muslin, 12

N
Napkin and Napkin Ring, 113
napkin rings, 113
napkins, 71, 113, 174
needlecases, 40, 224
needlecord, 12
needles, 8
Nightdress Case, 50
  template, 242
1950s Bistro Placemat, 210
  template, 252
Notebook Cover, 150

O
Oak Leaf Seat Cushion, 126
organdy, 12
organza, 12
oven mitts, 142

P
Pa Ndau Appliqué Box Lid,
  172
Pa Ndau Appliqué Frame, 170
  templates, 250
Padded Coat Hanger, 151
paisley motifs, 60
paper
  acid-free, 10
  carbon, 10, 24
  glue, 8
  graph, 10
  isometric, 10
  squared, 24
  squared dressmaker's, 10
  tissue, 10
  tracing, 10
patches
  backing papers, 19
  cutting out, 19
  joining, 20
  piercing, 20
  preparing, 19
  setting-in, 20
patchwork
  borders, 20
  box, 20
  equipment, 8
  fabrics, 12, 14–16
  log cabin, 21
  materials, 10
  sashing, 20
  techniques, 18–21
  templates, 18–19
Patchwork Bear, 44
Patchwork Cards, 116
Patchwork Cube, 126
Patchwork Curtain, 157
Patchwork Duffle Bag, 138
  templates, 249
Patchwork Frame, 88
Patchwork Tea and Egg
  Cosies, 112
Patchwork Toy Bag, 229
patterned fabrics, 16
pearl cotton, 10
Peg Bag, 192
  template, 251
Photo Frame, 117
pictures
  mounting, 25
  shadow, 54
  stretching, 25
piercing patches, 20
pillows, 126
  template, 248

pillowslips, 103, 234
pin cushions, 42, 121
pin tacking, 22
Pink-and-navy Quilt, 218
pinking shears, 8
pins, 8
place mats, 210
  template, 252
plastic templates, 19
playmats, 226
pockets, 61
poly vinyl chloride, 12
Pot Holder, 39
Pot Pourri Cushion, 186
  template, 250
pot pourri sachets, 130, 131
pouncing, 24
press studs, 10
Purple Zig Zag Cushion, 222
purses, 52, 187, 221
PVC, 12
PVC Bag, 240
  templates, 253
PVC Rucksack, 194
pyjamas, 61

Q
Quilted Box, 63
Quilted Egg Cosy, 169
Quilted Hat, 64
  template, 244–5
Quilted Pocket, 61
Quilted Waistcoat, 60
  template, 244
quilting
  basting, 21
  corded, 52
  equipment, 8
  fabrics, 12, 14–16
  hand, 21
  machine, 21
  materials, 10

pins, 8
shadow, 54
tacking, 21
techniques, 21
quilts, 36, 53, 66, 118, 124, 140, 141, 154, 182, 218

R
Rag Book, 96
rag dolls, 94
  template, 247
ribbon, 10
rotary cutter, 8
rucksacks, 104, 194
rulers, 8
running stitch, 23

S
safety pins, 8
San Blas Cushion, 144
San Blas Drawstring Bag, 145
San Blas Oven Mitts, 142
  template, 142
Sashiko Bag, 156
Sashiko Quilt, 154
sashing, 20
sateen, 12
satin, 12
Satin Duffel Bag, 220
Satin Handbag, 74
  templates, 245
scarves, 30, 89
Scatter Cushions, 202
scissors, 8
Scottie Dog T Shirt, 197
self edging, 90
Seminole Towel, 168
sequins, 10
set square, 8
setting-in, 20
Shadow Picture, 54
shadow quilting, 54
shantung, 12
sharp needles, 8

shears, 8
shirts, 61, 98, 197
Shoe Bag, 228
shoe bags, 99, 228
silhouettes, 55
silk, 12
Silk Christmas Cards, 204
Silk Dress, 74
Silken Bag, 70
Simple Patchwork Cushion Cover, 219
skirts, 74, 105
Slashed Silk Bag, 163
slip-stitch, 23
slippers, 31
Small Quilt, 124
Snakes and Ladders, 226
snap fasteners, 10
Square Linen Quilt, 36
squared dressmaker's paper, 10, 24
stab stitch, 23
Stained Glass Appliqué Cushion, 69
stitches, 23
  needles, 8
  unpickers, 8
stretching pictures, 25
String Patchwork Frame, 68

stuffing, 10
Suiting Throw, 47
Sunflower Shelf Edging, 90
sunflowers, 181
sweaters, 180
  template, 250

T
T-shirts 98, 197
Table Mats, 175
tablecloths, 72
tacking
  appliqué, 22
  pin, 22
  quilts, 21
  thread, 10
taffeta, 12
tailor's chalk, 8
tape measure, 8
tea cosies, 112
Teapot Cover, 38
techniques
  appliqué, 22
  patchwork, 18–21
  quilting, 21
  stitches, 23
teddy bears, 44
templates
  acetate, 19
  curved, 19
  making, 18–19
  projects, 242–53
  window, 19
textured fabrics, 16
thimbles, 8
thread, 10
  embroidery, 10
throws, 46, 47, 84, 110
  templates, 246
tissue paper, 10
tone, fabrics, 15
tools, 8
Toran Hanging, 208
towels, 168, 199, 252

Toy Bag, 106
tracing, 24
  paper, 10
transferring designs, 24
trapunto
  box, 62
  hat, 64
  purse, 52
  shadow picture, 54
Trapunto Box, 62
trimmings, 10

U
unpickers, 8

V
Valentine Card and Gift Tag, 213
vanishing marker, 8
velvet, 12
Velvet Scarf, 30
Velvet Slippers, 31
Velvet Throw, 46
voile, 12

W
wadding, 10
  tacking, 21
waistcoats, 60, 108, 132, 146, 216
  templates, 244, 248, 249
Wash Bag, 235
whip stitch, 23
window templates, 19
wool, 12
Wool Hat, 176

Y
yarn, 10

Z
zips, 10

ACKNOWLEDGEMENTS

· · · · · ·

The Publishers would like to thank the following craftspeople who designed and made the projects for this book: Abigail Barbier, Jenny Blair, Petra Boase, Louise Brownlow, Sally Burton, Julia Crook, Joanna Davies, Rachel Frost, Emma Ganderton, Lucinda Ganderton, Rachel Hyde, Judith Izatt, Sylvia Landers, Teresa Searle, Karen Spurgin, Isabel Stanley, Karen Triffitt, Chloe Walker, Jenny Watson, Angela Wheeler, Kate Whitworth, Dorothy Wood and Emma Woods. With thanks to Kay Dimbleby and her clients for permission to photograph the beautiful quilts she created on pages 29 b and 136 b. Additional photography by John Freeman, pages 29 b and 136 b; Debbie Patterson, pages 190 t and 191; Steve Tanner, pages 28, 29 t, 82 and 83; and Peter Williams, pages 136 t, 137 and 190 b.